DNA Fingerprinting

THE MEDICAL PERSPECTIVES SERIES

Advisors:

D.R. Harper *Department of Virology, Medical College of St Bartholomew's Hospital, London, U.K.*

Andrew P. Read *Department of Medical Genetics, University of Manchester, Manchester, U.K.*

Robin Winter *Institute of Child Health, London, U.K.*

Oncogenes and Tumor Suppressor Genes
Cytokines
The Human Genome
Autoimmunity
Genetic Engineering
Asthma
DNA Fingerprinting

Forthcoming titles:

Molecular Virology
HIV and AIDS
Human Vaccines and Vaccination
Antimicrobial Drug Action

DNA Fingerprinting

M. Krawczak and J. Schmidtke

Institut für Humangenetik, Medizinische Hochschule, 30623 Hannover,
Germany

BIOS
SCIENTIFIC
PUBLISHERS

© BIOS Scientific Publishers Limited, 1994

First published 1994

A CIP catalogue record for this book is available from the British Library.

ISBN 1 872748 43 0

BIOS Scientific Publishers Ltd
St Thomas House, Becket Street, Oxford OX1 1SJ, UK
Tel. +44 (0)865 726286. Fax +44 (0)865 246823

DISTRIBUTORS

Australia and New Zealand
   DA Information Services
   648 Whitehorse Road, Mitcham
   Victoria 3132

India
   Viva Books Private Limited
   4346/4C Ansari Road
   New Delhi 110 002

Singapore and South East Asia
   Toppan Company (S) PTE Ltd
   38 Liu Fang Road, Jurong
   Singapore 2262

USA and Canada
   Books International Inc.
   PO Box 605, Herndon, VA 22070

Typeset by Marksbury Typesetting Ltd, Midsomer Norton, Bath, UK.
Printed by Information Press Ltd, Oxford, UK.

Contents

Abbreviations

A	adenine
AmpFLP	amplification fragment length polymorphism
ASO	allele-specific oligonucleotide
C	cytosine
cDNA	complementary DNA
cM	centi-Morgan
dATP	deoxyadenosine 5'-triphosphate
dCTP	deoxycytidine 5'-triphosphate
DNA	deoxyribonucleic acid
2D-DNA typing	two-dimensional DNA typing
dGTP	deoxyguanosine 5'-triphosphate
dTTP	deoxythymidine 5'-triphosphate
HD	Huntington disease
HLA	human leukocyte antigen
HNPCC	hereditary nonpolyposis colorectal cancer
G	guanine
LINE	long interspersed nuclear elements
5mC	5-methylcytosine
mRNA	messenger RNA
MVR	minisatellite variant repeat
NRC	National Research Council
nt	nucleotide
ORF	open reading frame
PCR	polymerase chain reaction
PIC	polymorphism information content
RFLP	restriction fragment length polymorphism
RNA	ribonucleic acid
RSP	restriction site polymorphism
SD	standard deviation
SINE	short interspersed nuclear element
SSM	single step mutation
STR	short tandem repeats
T	thymine
U	uracil
VNTR	variable number of tandem repeats

Preface

Over the last 10 years, molecular genetics has evolved at a remarkable pace. Today, the genotypes of single cells can be determined at the level of the DNA, and even minute or degraded biological samples, useless for molecular analyses only a decade ago, have become amenable to accurate testing by means of sophisticated laboratory methods. This development has had an enormous practical impact on various scientific disciplines – from forensic medicine via parasitology to social biology – which aim to identify organisms or individuals on the basis of the material traces that they leave behind.

A major step forward in genetic identification was the realization that the repetitive sequence compartments of the genomes of virtually all species are highly polymorphic. These regions contain genetic loci comprising up to several hundred alleles, differing from each other with respect to length, sequence or both. When such polymorphisms are made visible, the emerging patterns in combination make up a unique feature of the analyzed individual, its 'DNA fingerprint'.

This book aims to provide an overview of DNA fingerprinting. We tried to pay equal attention to the molecular genetic basis of DNA polymorphism, its technical exploitation, and the statistical and ethical problems arising from its recruitment in medical and forensic practice. In a book such as this, it is of course impossible to provide a fully comprehensive review of a fast moving field of science. We therefore confined ourselves to describing the basics underlying DNA fingerprinting, illustrated by representative examples where appropriate, rather than compiling the immense body of information currently available on this topic.

We wish to thank everybody who has helped us in writing and improving this book. Special thanks are due to Ingolf Böhm, Jörg T. Epplen, Peter Nürnberg and David Hames for expert comments on the manuscript and proofs, the series advisors and BIOS for their continuing support and cooperation, and to Regina Krawczak and Bettina Pape for supreme patience and forbearance.

M. Krawczak
J. Schmidtke

Chapter 1

The genetic background

1.1 Genetic diversity and its substrate

Traditionally, the term 'fingerprint' refers to the patterns, which are highly characteristic for any human individual, of the ridged skin of the distal finger phalanges. For some years, the term 'fingerprinting' has also been used for the electrophoretic and chromatographic characterization of proteins and, more recently, of deoxyribonucleic acid (DNA) molecules. With DNA being the only basis of genetic differences between distinct organisms, DNA fingerprinting is presently the ultimate method of biological individualization.

This book concentrates on methods of determining the degree of relatedness of members of the same species, focusing on humans and occasionally glancing at other species, especially microorganisms, if medically relevant. A basic summary of the mutational and evolutionary mechanisms underlying the genetic diversity of individuals and species is also given.

In principle, genetic uniqueness is brought about by two factors: inheritance and new mutation. In diploid organisms, one genome is inherited from the father and the other from the mother. A process called meiotic recombination ensures that no offspring has a genome made up of a simple collection of entire grandparental chromosomes. Instead, chromosomes interchange genetic material at various points along the chromosome, mostly exchanging exactly corresponding segments between two homologous chromosomes so that the spatial organization of genes is unchanged. Therefore, an ancestral genome will never be reconstituted, even under extreme inbreeding. Genetic diversity is further sustained by spontaneous (i.e. environmentally induced) alteration of the genetic material, that is, by mutation. In haploid organisms, such as bacteria and viruses, equivalent processes exist by which the genetic material is shuffled around among members of a given population, and by which entirely new genetic traits can be formed.

1.1.1 Individualization by DNA sequencing

Since all genetic differences between individuals are laid down in the primary sequence of their genomic DNA, the most straightforward method of identifying an individual would be to determine this sequence for the genomes under comparison. However, with current technology, this is feasible only for small (e.g. some viral) genomes. A viral genome is typically composed of a DNA molecule measuring several thousand base pairs (bp) in length. A typical bacterial genome is about 1000 times longer, and the human genome is 1000 times the length of a bacterial genome. Even when equipped with the most sophisticated automated sequencing devices available at the time of writing this book, a single machine would still require more than 300 years to sequence an entire human genome fully.

However, depending on how densely spaced the DNA sequence differences between individual genomes actually are, it may suffice to sequence only a small proportion of a genome. Using the widely accepted estimate that two homologous chromosomes randomly drawn from the human population differ at a frequency of 1 in 300 bp, sequencing a 15 000 bp segment would guarantee that, with 99.9% probability, no pair of unrelated humans living on earth would be found to be identical. If the task were to decide, with the same nominal accuracy, whether an accused man is indeed the true father of a given child, only 4000 bp of DNA sequence would have to be determined for the child, the child's mother and the alleged father. While sequencing efforts on such a moderate scale appear to be routinely feasible, the practicality of this strategy still awaits experimental verification.

1.1.2 Genetic polymorphism and genetic individuality

Individualization by sequencing implies that comparatively long stretches of identical DNA must be screened before a difference can be expected to show up. A more efficient strategy is to limit the comparison to regions of the genome which are already known to differ frequently between individuals. Such regions are termed polymorphic sites. The concept of genetic polymorphism is fundamental to all current methods of determining genetic identity and relatedness, and therefore requires a more thorough discussion.

Genetic polymorphism is classically defined as the simultaneous occurrence in the same population of two or more discontinuous variants or genotypes. The frequencies of at least two of the types must be high enough so that they cannot be accounted for solely by recurrent mutation. Operationally, we may say that a polymorphism is a trait encoded by a piece of DNA (a locus) with two or more alleles (sequence variants), of which at least two occur at a frequency of more than 1% in a given population.

The first genetic polymorphism, discovered as early as 1900, was the ABO blood group system. This polymorphism, along with other subsequently discovered blood group, blood serum and other protein polymorphisms, was analyzed at the level of the gene product and not at that of the gene itself. Analysis at the gene level became feasible only after the introduction of genetic engineering into human genetics in the late 1970s and early 1980s. This new technology opened up the way to study a new class of polymorphic traits, namely those defined by the variation between one chromosome and another in the length of corresponding DNA fragments generated by digestion with restriction enzymes (Section 2.1.2).

The usefulness of genetic polymorphism for the definition of biochemical 'individuality' was realized immediately after the first 'individualities of metabolism' were discovered. The chance of an individual of European descent possessing the most frequent alleles of only 15 selected blood groups, serum proteins and red blood cell enzymes is about 1 in 20 000. With refinements in biochemical, immunological and molecular genetic technology, it is now easily possible to distinguish all living members of the human species at the protein and/or DNA level.

Such power of resolution is most effectively achieved by DNA probes that are capable of detecting in any individual a large number of highly polymorphic genetic loci simultaneously (DNA probes are small pieces of DNA that are complementary to the region to be analyzed). The term 'DNA fingerprinting' was introduced by Alec Jeffreys in 1985, to describe the barcode-like DNA fragment pattern generated by such multilocus probes (Section 2.2.3) after electrophoretic separation of genomic DNA fragments. Only later was this term also used to describe the combined use of several single-locus detection systems, this approach now being referred to as DNA profiling. In order to understand fully how these methods work in practice, we must first take a closer look at the basic techniques and achievements of molecular genetics.

1.2 The basics of molecular genetics

1.2.1 An historical review

The foundations of scientific genetics were laid in the second half of the nineteenth century: Charles Darwin recognized the principles of mutation and selection for speciation and evolution; Gregor Mendel discovered that heritable traits split up and recombine in an orderly manner when transmitted to offspring; Johann Friedrich Miescher first extracted and chemically analyzed nucleic acids; and Wilhelm Roux postulated that chromosomes are the carrier structures of inheritance. The era of molecular genetics (*Table 1.1*), however, did not start until 1944, when Oswald Theodore Avery and co-workers showed that DNA was the genetic material.

Table 1.1: Discoveries and technical developments in molecular genetics

Year	Researchers	Discovery
1944	Avery and co-workers	DNA is the genetic material
1945	Beadle and Tatum	One gene encodes one protein
1953	Watson and Crick	Structure of DNA and the genetic implications thereof
1961	Nirenberg and Matthaei	Deciphering of the genetic code
1972	Berg and co-workers	Molecular cloning of DNA
1977	Sanger and co-workers	Methods of DNA sequencing developed
1985	Jeffreys and co-workers	DNA fingerprinting developed

The current emphasis in human molecular genetics is on the mapping and sequencing of the entire human genome with the aim of better understanding the normal and pathological function of the genetic material, both at the individual and the population level. Further refinements of individualization techniques are a natural spin-off from this effort.

1.2.2 DNA is the genetic material

Until 1944, the material basis of inheritance was unknown. By removing polysaccharides and lipids from bacterial extracts and treating them with enzymes which degraded protein, ribonucleic acid (RNA) and DNA, Avery and co-workers were able to show that DNA is the substance by which a genetic trait can be transferred from one bacterial strain to another. To many researchers, including Avery himself, it was a great surprise that nucleic acids were not merely structural materials, as hitherto believed, but instead represented functionally important molecules. It was the seminal achievement of James Watson and Francis Crick to develop (in 1953) a model which combined existing physicochemical data on DNA structure with the requirements necessary for replicative and coding functions.

The discovery that DNA is the genetic material was a major surprise since it had formerly been believed that the phenotypic diversity exhibited by living organisms would require an underlying substrate of similar complexity. Proteins with their 20 different constituent subunits, the amino acids, appeared to be more likely candidates than DNA which consists of four elements only, the organic bases adenine (A), cytosine (C), guanine (G) and thymine (T). It soon became evident, however, that the stratagem of coding rests in the sequence of the elements.

Figure 1.1 shows that DNA is a polymeric molecule composed of two strands. Each strand consists of a 'backbone' of sugar (deoxyribose) and phosphate, with the bases A, C, G and T attached to the backbone and pointing towards the center of the double-stranded molecule. Hydrogen bonds are formed between the bases of opposite strands: A always pairs with T, G always pairs with C. Facing A:T and G:C conformations are called base pairs. A proper chemical structural formula of a section (5'-ACGT-3') of the DNA molecule is given on the right side of *Figure 1.1*. The 5' and 3' refer to the numbering of the carbon atoms in the deoxyribose ring – the 5' atom of each sugar points towards one end of the DNA strand, and the 3' atom towards the other.

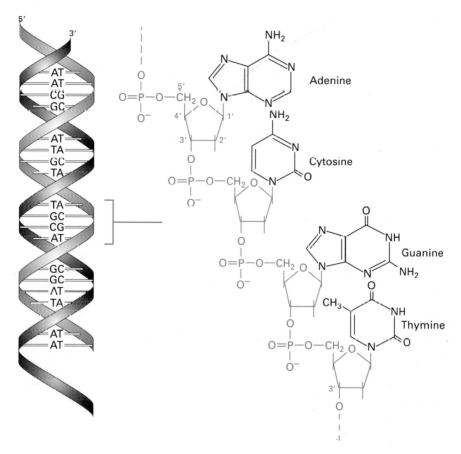

Figure 1.1: The structure of DNA. On the left-hand side is shown a diagram of a double-stranded DNA molecule in which the sugar–phosphate backbone of each strand is represented by a ribbon. This illustrates that the base-paired strands actually generate a helical conformation – the double helix. Reproduced from Gelehrter and Collins (1990) *Principles of Medical Genetics*, with permission from Williams & Wilkins.

1.2.3 Gene expression

A gene is classically defined as a stretch of DNA that encodes a specific polypeptide. Most genes in eukaryotes consist of coding sequences (called exons) separated by noncoding regions (introns). When a gene of a higher organism is to be expressed, it is transcribed to yield an RNA copy of the exon and intron sequences. This primary RNA transcript is then processed to yield messenger RNA (mRNA), which contains only exon sequences. The mRNA is then 'translated' by ribosomes to generate the specific encoded polypeptide (see *Figure 1.2*). Every three bases in the mRNA (a codon) specifies one amino acid, with uracil (U) replacing thymine in DNA.

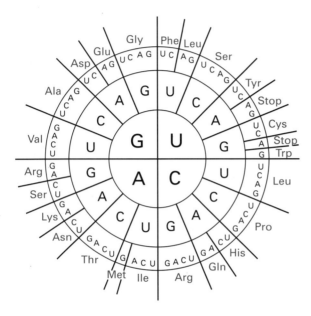

Figure 1.2: The 'rising sun' diagram of the genetic code. Three bases in mRNA encode one amino acid. Codons must be read from the center (5′) to the periphery (3′). His(tidine), for example, is encoded by CAC or CAU. Since the first amino acid of all newly synthesized polypeptides is methionine, AUG is called the initiation codon when it serves this role. UAA, UAG and UGA do not encode amino acids and hence terminate translation. These are therefore called termination, or stop, codons.

Any mutational change observable at the level of the protein (e.g. variation in enzymes or serum proteins, or in the highly individual tissue types determined by the human leukocyte antigen (HLA) genes, as well as disease-causing alterations) is due to an alteration in the codons at the level of the DNA. Not every mutational change in coding DNA, however, leads to an altered protein product. As can be inferred from *Figure 1.2*, most amino acids are encoded redundantly. The codon CUA may mutate to CUC, CUG, CUU, UUA or UUG, and will still encode the same amino acid, leucine. Thus, in coding regions, far less polymorphism is to be expected at the protein than at the DNA level.

Both the transcriptional and the translational processes require the interaction of enzymes and certain RNAs that are themselves end products of the genes by which they are encoded: small nuclear RNAs, ribosomal RNAs and transfer RNAs. Some of these protein and RNA constituents regulate gene action in time and space. They help to determine which gene is to be expressed in which cell at a given developmental stage, whilst others are constituent molecules of the translation machinery.

1.2.4 Chromosomes

If stretched out, the DNA of a single human cell would extend approximately 2 m in length. In order to fit into the cell nucleus with a diameter about five orders of magnitude smaller, DNA needs to be efficiently packed. The end product of an elaborate compaction of DNA with structurally and functionally relevant proteins is the chromosome. Every species has a characteristic set of chromosomes in each cell, called the karyotype. The human karyotype consists of 46 chromosomes. Out of these, 44 chromosomes form homologous pairs (one from each parent) and, in addition, females have two X chromosomes and males have one X and one Y chromosome per cell. The Y chromosome is passed from fathers to their sons and contains the genetic information which makes the embryo develop as a male; without a Y chromosome a mammalian embryo develops as a female.

1.2.5 Mitosis

In higher organisms, most body cells have life spans shorter than that of the overall organism. Therefore, there is a need to create new and regenerate old cells. In a process called *mitosis* (*Figure 1.3*), a somatic cell divides to give rise to two daughter cells. During mitosis, the nuclear DNA is replicated and each daughter strand is compacted and packed by the chromosomal proteins. Just before the cell actually divides, the duplicated chromosomes, composed of two so-called sister chromatids, become visible under the microscope. Chromosomes line up along the equatorial disk of the cell, divide at the centromere, and are pulled, one chromatid each, into the emerging daughter cells.

1.2.6 Meiosis (gametogenesis)

The mature germ cells of diploid organisms such as humans must contain only a single (haploid) genome; otherwise, the genome size would double in each generation when sperm and egg fuse to make the zygote. This reduction in number is combined with a process designed to mix up the genetic material in the offspring by random separation and recombination

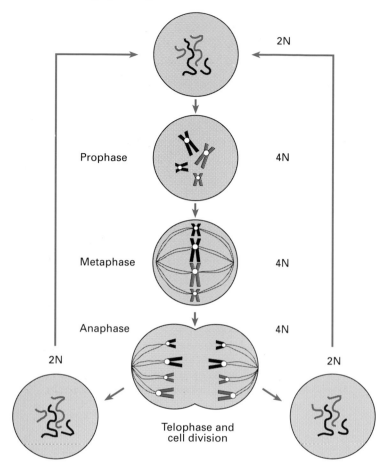

Figure 1.3: Mitosis (somatic cell division). For simplicity only four chromosomes, consisting of two pairs of autosomes, are shown. The 'ploidy' of the cell is shown at each stage: 2N represents the diploid state. After formation of sister chromatids but before cell division, the cell contains an amount of DNA corresponding to 4N.

of homologous chromosomes. The genesis of germ cells, termed *meiosis*, can be divided into two stages (*Figure 1.4*): meiosis I and meiosis II. In meiosis I the diploid chromosome set of the progenitor cell replicates just as in mitosis, but the sister chromatids do not separate. The homologous duplicated chromosomes line up in pairs, form chiasmata (contacts or bridges) and (normally) exchange homologous material between nonsister chromatids in a process called crossing-over (*Figure 1.5*). An uneven number of cross-overs between two loci results in a recombination of their constituent genetic material. At the final stage of meiosis I, the chromosomes move to opposite poles, where the sister chromatids separate in meiosis II. The result is a set of 23 chromosomes per germ cell (sperm or ovum), with each chromosome being a patchwork of two parental chromosomes, and with each cell carrying a random permutation of the parental complements.

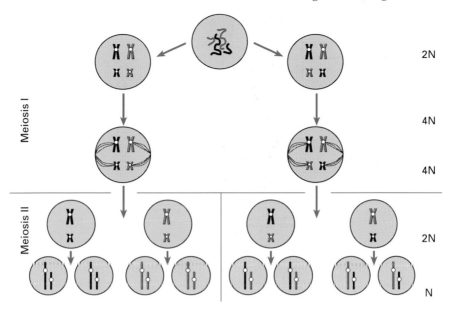

Figure 1.4: Meiosis (germ cell division). Only two pairs of autosomes are shown. As a result of the first meiotic division, each cell retains only one partner from each homologous pair. Their distribution in the daughter cells is completely random so that, in the example shown, two alternative meiotic pathways are possible after metaphase I. Meiosis II, which is essentially a mitotic division performed by half the genetic material, leads to sister chromatid separation. For simplicity, cross-overs between chromatids are not shown.

1.2.7 Replication and mutation

The complementarity of the two DNA strands guarantees that each contains a complete copy of the information carried in the DNA molecule. When cells divide, the genetic information to be passed on to the daughter cells must be copied. Each strand can serve as a template for the synthesis of a new complementary strand. This process of replication is dependent on the auxiliary action of enzymes, with DNA polymerases playing a central role. In view of its tremendous speed – around 30 bases replicated per second by vertebrate DNA polymerase α – this process is astonishingly accurate. Only one base in 10^6 of the DNA sequence is replicated incorrectly, and most of these errors are subsequently corrected. For example, of guanines wrongly incorporated instead of an adenine opposite a thymine, only 0.1% or less go unrecognized by the proof-reading mechanism built into each replicative cell. The remaining 1 in 10^8–10^{11} bases in which mother and daughter cells eventually differ defines what is known as the point mutation rate.

In looking at mutations only at the molecular level, we have not yet considered that, for a mutation to survive, it must still stand the test of selection. Selection, however, acts on the phenotype rather than the genotype, and as we will see in Section 1.2.8, a huge proportion of the

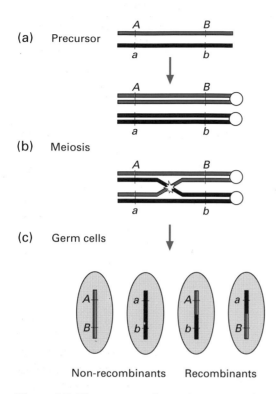

(a)   Precursor

(b)   Meiosis

(c)   Germ cells

Non-recombinants   Recombinants

Figure 1.5. The process of crossing-over and recombination. (a) The precursor of a germ cell contains alleles 'A' and 'B' arranged in one haplotype, and 'a' and 'b' in the other. (b) A cross-over event takes place between two of the nonsister chromatids and results in two novel haplotypes, Ab and aB. (c) After meiosis has been completed, two germ cells (i.e. one half) contain one of the new haplotypes whereas the other two germ cells contain the original haplotypes. Reproduced from Ref. [1].

genome is probably quite irrelevant to the phenotype. These extragenic compartments represent the bulk of the genome in higher organisms, and exhibit effective mutation rates identical or close to the rate intrinsic to the DNA replication machinery. However, the important regions of the genome which are responsible for the shaping of the phenotype are more sensitive to change. For example, a mutation leading to the loss of expression of a vital protein-encoding gene is usually lethal, although a minor fraction of mutations leading to amino acid substitutions may prove advantageous. Nevertheless, coding genes normally have much lower effective mutation rates than noncoding portions of the genome (*Table 1.2*).

At the level of the DNA, diversity is generated not only by single base substitutions but also by the loss (deletion), gain (insertion, duplication), and rearrangement (e.g. inversion) of variable lengths of sequence. The molecular mechanisms underlying these alterations (see Section 3.2) are

Table 1.2: Effective point mutation rates in the human genome

Source/gene	Point mutation rate per nucleotide per generation
Bulk DNA	4.4×10^{-8}
Coagulation factor IX gene	3.2×10^{-9}
Ornithine transcarbamylase gene	7.5×10^{-10}

See Ref. [1], p. 321, for references.

different from those causing base substitutions, and also strike at different rates – in some very special cases they occur at rates which are orders of magnitude higher than the base substitution rate in genes. Many loci contributing to standard DNA fingerprints are characterized by an exceptionally high liability to mutations of this type. In part, this high liability is both due to and reflected by the sort of polymorphism they bear, namely a dramatic inter-individual variability in the number of short repeat units arranged in a tandem fashion.

1.2.8 Nuclear and mitochondrial DNA

In most organisms, including bacteria and humans, the genetic information resides in more than one cellular compartment. Whereas the bulk of the genetic information is to be found in the cell nucleus or its equivalent, some can also be found in organelles other than the nucleus, such as plasmids (prokaryotes), chloroplasts (plants) and mitochondria (eukaryotes).

The human genome has a large nuclear and a small mitochondrial component (*Figure 1.6*). The size of the nuclear genome is approximately 3×10^9 bp, whereas the mitochondrial genome in human cells is a single circular DNA molecule, only 16 569 bp in length. However, since there is usually only one nucleus as opposed to often several thousand mitochondria in a single cell, up to 0.5% of total cellular DNA is mitochondrial. Mitochondrial DNA is characterized by a point mutation rate 6–17 times higher than nuclear DNA, probably because it lacks efficient DNA repair mechanisms. Thus, due to its low complexity and its high cellular redundancy, mitochondrial DNA is easy to analyze; its high mutation rate makes it extremely variable. It is not, however, generally suitable for the determination of kinship, because mitochondrial DNA is almost strictly maternally inherited in humans (sperm contribute hardly any mitochondria to the zygote). Thus, mitochondrial DNA is entirely useless in, for example, paternity testing.

Almost all of the mitochondrial DNA encodes genes, specifying either polypeptides or RNA products including ribosomal and transfer RNA. There are 37 such genes in the human mitochondrial genome. In nuclear DNA, gene and gene-related sequences comprise about one-fifth of the total DNA sequence, although less than 10% of this is actually coding. Estimates of the number of genes range from 50 000 to 100 000. The majority of nuclear DNA is noncoding, and is found either within

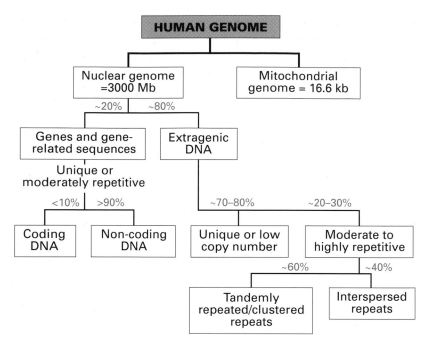

Figure 1.6: Organization of the human genome. Reproduced from Strachan (1992) *The Human Genome*, BIOS Scientific Publishers.

genes, as introns (see Section 1.2.3), or between genes with no known function. The former is called intragenic DNA whilst the latter is extragenic DNA.

Some stretches of this apparent 'junk' DNA are unique, which means that they occur only once per haploid genome. Others are present in various numbers of copies (repetitive sequences) (*Figure 1.6*). In total, about one-third of the genome consists of repetitive sequences. Although most coding genes are unique, some are also repetitive and may exhibit more or less pronounced sequence differences between individual elements, thus forming gene families.

1.3 The molecular organization of the human genome

1.3.1 Information storage and genome size

The amount of information a DNA molecule can potentially store is enormous. As in any other language, it is the order of the letters and groups of letters ('words') that confers meaning on the sequence. In the language of the DNA, there are 4^n different words of length n, and a comprehensive collection of DNA words of the same length as the word 'information' would fill 100 king-sized dictionaries. As in every other language, of course, not every word that can be formed makes sense. As already pointed out in Section 1.2.8, only small fractions of the genomes of higher organisms actually do make sense (i.e. encode proteins and the elements necessary for their qualitatively and quantitatively correct synthesis). The bulk of DNA, probably 98% in the case of human DNA, does not appear to have any sequence-dependent function. Whatever its biological role may be, this DNA follows the same rules of inheritance as the remainder, and can therefore be used to identify species and individuals.

How much DNA is actually present in the genome? A glance at *Table 1.3* shows that genome sizes vary considerably between different organisms. It can be inferred that, for small genome sizes, there is a good correlation between DNA content and complexity of an organism. In the upper size region, however, this relationship no longer holds true. Why should a newt need 20 times more genetic information than a herring? Since it appears very unlikely that amphibians and plants have demands for coding potential that we have not yet noticed, we may assume that noncoding sequences have accumulated more dramatically as genomes grew larger during evolution and/or that many or even all biological functions are encoded redundantly in the very large genomes due to, for example, recent polyploidization.

Table 1.3: Genome sizes of various species

Species	DNA content (bp)
Small virus (SV40)	5×10^3
Bacterial virus (lambda phage)	5×10^4
Very large virus (Vaccinia virus)	2×10^5
Escherichia coli (bacterium)	4×10^6
Saccharomyces cerevisiae (yeast)	2×10^7
Caenorhabditis elegans (nematode)	5×10^7
Drosophila melanogaster (fly)	1×10^8
Clupea harengus (fish)	1×10^9
Homo sapiens (mammal)	3×10^9
Allium cepa (plant)	1.5×10^{10}
Triturus cristatus (newt)	2×10^{10}

1.3.2 Genome architecture

The genome constituents mentioned in Section 1.2.8 (i.e. coding and non-coding, unique and repetitive sequences), are arranged in a highly complex fashion. In higher genomes, most genes are mosaic-like structures of coding DNA (exons) and noncoding DNA (introns), the latter being removed ('spliced out') from the initial transcript when this is processed into mRNA. A very simple human gene, β-globin, which exhibits an exon–intron pattern is depicted in *Figure 1.7*. Why genes have evolved this mosaic structure remains a mystery. A popular view holds that exons represent primordial functional building blocks shuffled together when complex genes evolved. Introns may be involved in regulating the

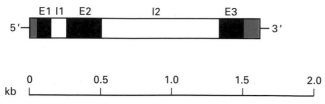

Figure 1.7: Structure of the human β-globin gene. This gene is 1.6 kb long, which is the average size of human genes (although some human genes extend for megabases while others are much shorter). Black blocks are exons (coding portions), open blocks are introns (noncoding portions), and orange blocks are 5′ and 3′ regions (found in mature RNA but not translated into protein).

expression of the surrounding protein coding sequence, or they may themselves contain one or more other different genes, again with or without introns. Introns can be unique or contain repetitive DNA.

With only a small proportion of genomic DNA actually coding, genes on chromosomes should be thought of as fertile oases in the seemingly functionless desert of the genome. The bulk of intergenic DNA is unique or low copy, but large areas of this desert are repetitive. Both the unique and the repetitive components of intergenic DNA (and also of introns) are valuable resources of genetic polymorphism. This is because there appear to be no constraints on introducing and maintaining sequence changes, as long as there is no function (such as maintaining the integrity of chromosomal structure) that can be impeded by such changes.

Repetitive DNA can be further subdivided, both with respect to the degree of repetition and with respect to the relative location of the elements of a repeat. Repeat families comprise a continuum of copy numbers per genome, from just a few up to millions. Genetic polymorphism is partly caused by variable numbers of elements at a given repetitive locus, and repeat families differ from one another in the way their elements are arranged in the genome. The latter can be usefully divided into tandem repeats and interspersed repeats.

1.3.3 Tandem repeats

Repetitive sequence elements which are arranged in tandem are known as satellite, minisatellite and microsatellite sequences. The reason for borrowing a word from astronomy in order to describe a class of DNA sequences is a historical one, the initial method of separating such sequences from the rest of the genome was buoyant density gradient centrifugation, by which DNA with a base composition very different from the bulk of the genome manifests itself in minor ('satellite') banding components. Currently, the three terms refer to different levels of repetition and different repeat unit length (*Table 1.4*).

Satellite DNA is dispersed over almost the entire genome. Satellites, minisatellites and microsatellites can be highly variable and thus form

Table 1.4: Definition of tandemly repeated (satellite) DNA

Type	Degree of repetition (per locus)	Number of loci	Repeat unit length (bp)
Satellite	10^3–10^7	1–2 per chromosome	One to several thousand
Minisatellite	10–10^3	Many thousands per genome	9–100
Microsatellite	10–10^2	Up to 10^5 per genome depending on repeat motif	1–6

excellent tools for genetic individualization. Their variability is most often due to particular arrays on a given chromosome having different repeat numbers in different people. Thus, they form allelic variants and for a number of mini- and microsatellites almost every individual is heterozygous. Polymorphisms created by such elements are termed variable number of tandem repeat (VNTR) polymorphisms.

The nomenclature adopted in *Table 1.4* follows that of Tautz [2]. In the literature, the use of terminology is not uniform and is sometimes rather confusing. Minisatellites are sometimes equated with VNTRs, but VNTR is a term applicable to all repeat classes. Microsatellites are occasionally referred to as 'simple' sequences or short tandem repeats (STRs), but STR is also used for synthetic tandem repeat probes capable of detecting minisatellite sequences.

Polymorphism due to variation in the number of elements within a given array is thought to be generated during DNA replication, for example by the mutational process of slipped strand mispairing (see Section 3.2.2). In addition to allelic variation in repeat number, polymorphism at mini- and microsatellite loci can also be caused by sequence changes in the vicinity of these repeats. Finally, a novel approach aims at exploiting variation within the repeat units of different minisatellite alleles; this is known as minisatellite variant repeat–polymerase chain reaction (MVR–PCR) or 'digital' fingerprinting (see Section 2.2.1).

1.3.4 Interspersed repeats

In the nuclear DNA of humans and most other eukaryotes, repetitive sequences can be found that are not organized in tandem arrays but are more or less regularly interspersed with unique DNA sequences throughout the genome. The Alu and Kpn repeat families are representative examples of short and long interspersed nuclear elements, known as SINEs and LINEs, respectively. In evolutionary terms, they have probably contributed to genetic differences between species and individuals by playing a role in retrotransposition events (see Section 3.2.1) and in promoting unequal crossing-over.

References

1. Cooper, D.N. and Krawczak, M. (1993) *Human Gene Mutation*. BIOS Scientific Publishers, Oxford.
2. Tautz, D. (1993) in *DNA Fingerprinting: State of the Science* (S.D.J. Pena, R. Chakraborty, J.T. Epplen and A.J. Jeffreys, eds). Birkhäuser Verlag, Basel, pp. 21–28.

Further reading

Williams, J., Ceccarelli, A. and Spurr, N. (1993) *Genetic Engineering*. BIOS Scientific Publishers, Oxford.

Chapter 2

Studying DNA polymorphism

2.1 The analytical tools

Molecular biology, probably the fastest expanding field of life science in our time, has developed a large variety of methods designed to study structural and functional properties of genes and genomes. In the context of this book, we shall restrict ourselves to the techniques used to reveal and study genetic polymorphisms.

2.1.1 Extracting genomic DNA

Obviously, the first step in characterizing a biological sample at the level of the genome is to purify its DNA (*Figure 2.1*). The nuclear DNA of higher organisms is compacted with proteins into chromatin – the material which constitutes chromosomes. DNA is extracted simply by removing the other components of the chromatin. This is achieved mainly by the action of enzymes, protein-denaturing agents, salt and organic solvents such as phenol and chloroform. Depending on what quality of DNA is required (high or low molecular weight, double- or single-stranded), some purification steps can be omitted or simplified so that extracting crude DNA may take only a matter of minutes. The source of DNA can be any biological sample containing nucleated cells, such as blood (the white cells are nucleated), semen, hair, bones, saliva (mouth epithelial cells), and urine containing epithelial cells from the kidney and the urinary tract. If a prenatal analysis is required, amniotic fluid, chorionic villus cells, or fetal blood can be used.

Fresh cells are a source of high molecular weight DNA, which is usually required for applying DNA probes that hybridize to many spatially dispersed polymorphisms simultaneously (multilocus probes; see Section 2.2.3). Many other biological samples and remains contain degraded DNA which can nevertheless be investigated by enzymatic

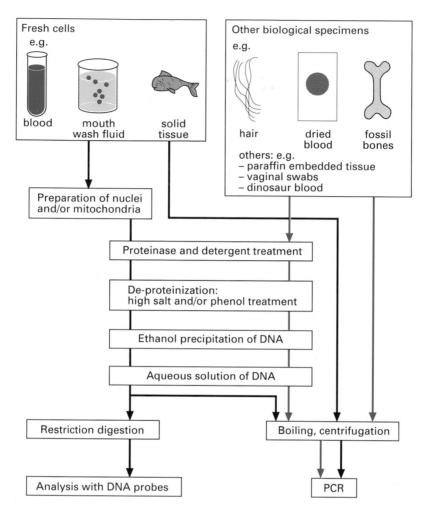

Figure 2.1: Extraction and processing of DNA.

amplification of DNA (Section 2.1.7). The corresponding experimental protocols require little more than boiled tissue, freed from cellular debris by a short centrifugation step.

Whereas short stretches of DNA are remarkably stable, the huge molecules that constitute chromosomal DNA (up to hundreds of megabases) are very fragile and are easily broken into smaller fragments by mechanical shearing or enzymatic attack (within hours or days, depending on temperature and other variables). Nevertheless, since natural degradation of DNA is more or less random, large DNA molecules often remain, even after a considerable time, provided the original biological sample was large enough. Thus, it is almost always worth trying to extract DNA from any biological remains, be it a blood stain or a piece of bone from the site of an assault, a shred of skin of a 1000-year-old mummy, a formalin-fixed sample from a pathologist's shelves, or a hair curl inherited from a presumptive ancestor. Some of the techniques outlined below will be particularly useful when only badly degraded DNA is available.

Another practical problem arises when the biological material from which DNA is to be extracted stems from a mixture of sources. If it is not possible to separate cells or tissues, DNA is extracted from the mixed sample, and differentiation according to source has to take place at the level of genotyping. Bacterial contamination is usually not a problem, because detection systems that work on human or bacterial DNA rarely cross-react. If contamination is by tissues from other higher organisms, problems may arise, especially with multilocus probes (Section 2.2.3) since most of these will hybridize to DNA sequences which are present in various organisms and will thus cross-react with a wide variety of species. Finally, if the biological sample is a mixture of cells from two or more human individuals (such as mingled blood spots on a suspect's clothes), typing methods are required that allow unambiguous identification of the individual contributions.

There are a number of ways in which a DNA sample can be processed further. Quality of the sample permitting, it could be characterized directly – for example, after restriction analysis and Southern or dot blot hybridization (Sections 2.1.4 and 2.1.5). Another option could be to enhance the sample, quantitatively and qualitatively, by *in vitro* or *in vivo* amplification procedures (Section 2.1.7).

2.1.2 Restriction enzymes

Restriction enzymes cut double-stranded DNA at short recognition sequences, usually spanning 4–8 nucleotides (nt), which are specific for each enzyme. For example, restriction endonuclease *Alu*I will cut DNA whenever it encounters the sequence AGCT, *Eco*RI will cut at GAATTC, and *Not*I will cleave at GCGGCCGC. In principle, the spacing of these recognition sites in the genome should be random but, of course, their occurrence depends on the precise sequence of the DNA being examined. Thus, the size distribution of human DNA cleaved by restriction enzymes will range from less than 1 kb to several megabases, and the number of different fragments generated from human nuclear DNA by the action of these enzymes will vary from thousands to millions.

When cleaved DNA is size-separated by electrophoresis on a track length of, say, 10–20 cm and made visible by staining with a fluorescent dye, the whole range of fragment sizes will manifest itself as a smear of DNA. Specific fragments can be visualized only by probing the restricted genomic DNA with complementary molecules. The basic principle of this technique is outlined in the next section.

2.1.3 Technological exploitation of DNA strand complementarity

A specific single-stranded piece of DNA will base pair only to its complementary strand, even in extremely complex mixtures of molecules.

In vitro, this ability of complementary single-stranded DNA molecules to anneal is used in molecular hybridization reactions. The principle of molecular hybridization is fundamental to almost all DNA analysis techniques. The specificity of the annealing reaction is dependent on the experimental conditions, including the salt concentration and the temperature of the reaction mix. When the conditions are carefully controlled, a single-stranded DNA molecule of 15 nt (an oligonucleotide) will easily find its exact counterpart in a mixture of DNA sequences that has up to 200 million times its sequence complexity (e.g. the human genome).

2.1.4 Southern blotting

The now classical method of visualizing specific DNA fragments was developed in 1975 by Edwin Southern (*Figure 2.2*). In this basic procedure, the test DNA is digested with one or more restriction enzymes, size-fractionated by agarose gel electrophoresis, denatured (i.e. experimentally treated so that the molecules become single-stranded), and transferred to a solid membrane for hybridization.

More specifically, the negatively charged DNA fragments move from the cathode to the anode during electrophoresis, and smaller fragments move faster than larger ones ('molecular sieving'). After electrophoresis, the DNA fragments are denatured by exposing the gel to an alkaline solution. In the actual Southern blotting procedure, the DNA fragments are transferred from the wet gel on to solid membranes where they become immobilized at their precise gel positions.

After the DNA has become fixed on the membrane, it is incubated with the labeled probe, a small DNA molecule complementary to the target sequence of interest. This incubation takes place under controlled experimental conditions (e.g. salt concentration and temperature) for a few hours, allowing the probe to find its blotted counterpart. Any excess probe and nonspecifically bound probe is washed off after hybridization. If the probe has been radioactively labeled, an X-ray film is put on to the membrane and, after exposure, the pattern of DNA fragments which are homologous to (and hence have hybridized to) the radioactive probe becomes visible on the film as a collection of dark bands.

In recent years, many variations of this basic scheme have been proposed. Re-useable nylon and other membranes have been developed; the blotting step itself can be skipped if very short DNA probes capable of penetrating a dried gel are used; radioactive substances can be replaced by labeling and detection systems based on immunological or color reactions or chemiluminescence.

2.1.5 Dot blotting

Southern blotting and related procedures yield two types of information simultaneously: information about the presence of a particular DNA

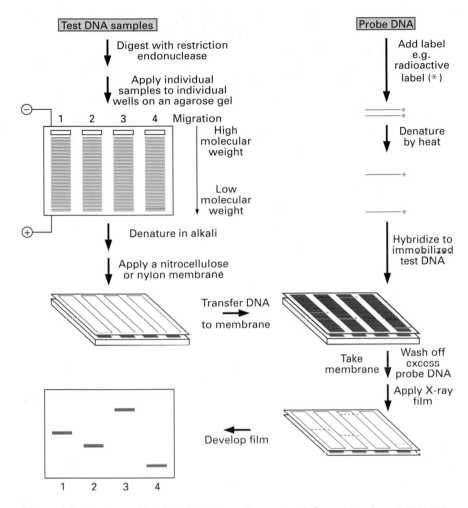

Figure 2.2: Southern blot hybridization. Reproduced from Strachan (1992) *The Human Genome*, BIOS Scientific Publishers Ltd.

fragment, and a measure of its size. However, if we are interested only in whether a particular sequence is present or not in the tested DNA, a much simpler method exists called dot blotting. With this technique, an aliquot of denatured DNA is spotted on to a membrane, and subsequent hybridization with a sequence-specific probe yields the required information when a suitable detection system is applied.

2.1.6 Generation of DNA probes

DNA probes can be generated in many ways, depending on the type of probe required. The simplest is to generate human DNA clones more or less randomly. To do this, fragments of human DNA are integrated into bacterial vectors (which can replicate in bacteria). As a result, whenever the virus replicates so does the human DNA, in the form of hybrid molecules. The resulting clones are usually picked at random and evaluated on DNA bound to a Southern blot (*Figure 2.2*). If the clone happens to contain a unique sequence, one or a few autoradiographic bands will show up, depending on which restriction enzymes have been used to cut the tested DNA. More bands will be detected (sometimes too many, resulting in a smear), if the clone happens to contain a repeat element.

Subsequently, the chromosomal origin of clones can be determined by probing panels of somatic cell hybrids, each containing a different subset of human chromosomes on a nonhuman background (e.g. from hamster or mouse). Alternatively, hybridization to metaphase chromosome spreads allows the localization of the probe *in situ*. A possible function of the cloned sequence can be suggested by sequencing the DNA and using the genetic code to deduce the sequence of the encoded protein.

Often, the primary reason for molecular cloning is not to generate random probes but rather to investigate a particular gene. Then other means must be sought in order to clone specifically the desired DNA sequence. A common way is by using information about the protein sequence (if that information is already available) to deduce the likely coding DNA sequence and then synthesize this DNA sequence for use as a probe.

Like many other naturally occurring substances, DNA can also be synthesized *in vitro*. Less than 20 years after Keichi Itakura's pioneering work in this field, DNA synthesis has become cheap and commonplace. Today, it is routinely performed by laboratory robots, which only require the sequence to be generated, and then within minutes add one nucleotide to each growing DNA oligonucleotide chain. Such synthetic oligonucleotides, measuring 12 nt or more, can be used directly to probe genomic DNA or can be used to prime polymerase chain reactions and DNA sequencing (Sections 2.1.7 and 2.1.8).

It has already been mentioned (Section 1.1.2) that, in the 'premolecular' era of biology, polymorphisms could be studied only at the level of the protein and were thus restricted to coding regions. In addition to investigating exactly the same polymorphisms again, now at the level of the DNA, polymorphisms have become available which do not result in amino acid substitutions at all; that is, they are variants which are 'same sense' due to the redundancy of the genetic code. However, it should be noted in the context of DNA fingerprinting that the examination of polymorphism within or very close to coding genes will sometimes reveal excess information, allowing unwanted inference about personal features of the individual under study (see Section 6.2).

2.1.7 The polymerase chain reaction

The polymerase chain reaction (PCR) is a novel and extremely powerful method that allows selective amplification *in vitro* of specific target DNA sequences from large, heterogeneous sources such as genomic DNA. The principle of PCR is outlined in *Figure 2.3*. In order to be able to select a particular target from a mixture of sequences, specific sequence information must be available. This information is used to synthesize short oligonucleotides (primers; typically 20–25 nt) that initially bind to the complementary sequences in a molecular hybridization reaction.

At the start of the process, all reaction partners must be single-stranded, which is achieved by heat-denaturation ('melting'). The reaction mixture also contains the DNA building blocks, the four deoxynucleoside triphosphates dATP, dCTP, dGTP and dTTP. DNA polymerase is then added, which synthesizes a complementary strand by connecting the deoxynucleoside triphosphates according to the sequence information given by the template strand. The specificity of the PCR reaction derives from the fact that DNA polymerase is unable to start a completely new

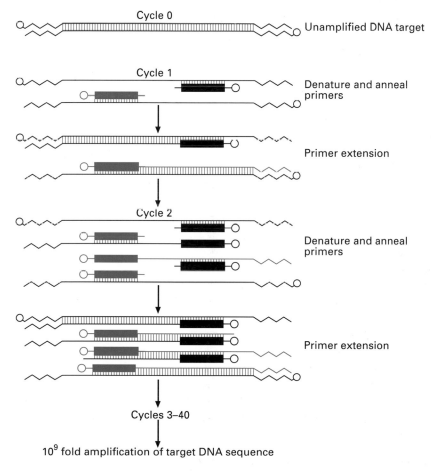

Figure 2.3: The polymerase chain reaction. Reproduced from Cooper and Krawczak (1993) *Human Gene Mutation*, BIOS Scientific Publishers Ltd.

strand; it can only extend the primer sequence. Subsequently, the newly formed double-stranded DNA molecules are heat-denatured again, and can themselves serve as templates in a new cycle of DNA synthesis.

Each cycle consists of three steps: (1) annealing primer molecules to the template DNA; (2) elongating the nascent strand; and (3) melting the double-stranded molecules to form two new single-stranded templates. During each step, the temperature and duration of the reaction must be carefully controlled, which is most easily achieved by using an automated device. One cycle will normally require only a few (typically 2–5) minutes, depending on the equipment used. The DNA polymerase used is one chosen for its heat stability, so that it survives the heating step of the cycle. The final result is that only the DNA sequence located between the two primers is eventually synthesized. After approximately 30 cycles this DNA sequence is theoretically amplified a billion times. In practice, however, much less DNA is synthesized, although the end result is usually still visible to the naked eye on an analytical agarose gel.

Whereas it is comparatively easy to use PCR to synthesize DNA molecules measuring up to a few hundred base pairs, it becomes progressively more difficult to produce larger molecules. The upper limit, using present-day technology, is approximately 10 kb. On the other hand, the method is extremely robust in that it works with small amounts of DNA, and functions even if the DNA is badly degraded. Thus, the starting material may consist of a single cell, and biological samples have been examined that were dried, mummified, buried, embedded in amber or stored in paraffin blocks. PCR methodology has been applied to both single-copy and repetitive sequences. It is the method of choice for the visualization of microsatellites, but it has also been employed successfully to amplify minisatellite alleles.

2.1.8 DNA sequencing

The majority of biological individuality is ultimately defined by the sequence of the genomic DNA. Thus, the most direct (although not the most efficient) way of determining identity would be to establish this sequence over a stretch long enough to differ, due to intermittent variation, from that of everybody else.

The most popular method of DNA sequencing, designed by Fred Sanger in 1977, is in many ways related to PCR. Both methods mimic DNA replication in that DNA polymerase is used to synthesize a new double-stranded DNA molecule from a primer molecule and the instructions given by the single-stranded DNA template. The method of DNA sequencing, however, incorporates two artificial tricks. The normal nucleotides are mixed with small amounts of their dideoxy analogs which, when incorporated, lead to immediate chain termination. Secondly, at least one of the nucleotides is radioactively labeled. Four reactions are set up simultaneously, differing only by which of the four dideoxynucleotides is added. These reactions are allowed to proceed for some time and are then loaded on to a denaturing gel made of polyacrylamide. In each reaction, the dideoxynucleotides are incorporated into the growing DNA molecules at random, with each nucleotide on the new strand having the same chance of occasionally being substituted by a dideoxy (chain-terminating) nucleotide. Therefore, size separation of the reaction products results in a ladder of bands from which the original nucleotide sequence can be read directly.

2.1.9 The allele-specific oligonucleotide (ASO) approach

A very useful combination of molecular genetic techniques is to integrate PCR, dot blotting and oligonucleotide probing in the allele-specific oligonucleotide (ASO) approach. The very short DNA duplexes formed by perfectly matching oligonucleotides of 15–20 nt hybridized to genomic DNA or PCR-amplified DNA are stable only under highly specific conditions of temperature and salt concentration. Under such hybridization conditions, even a single mismatch will prevent the oligonucleotide from binding in detectable amounts to the target DNA. *Figure 2.4* shows how this methodology can be applied to detect polymorphisms caused by single base pair changes. This method in particular lends itself to automation, because every step is mechanically simple and easily controlled.

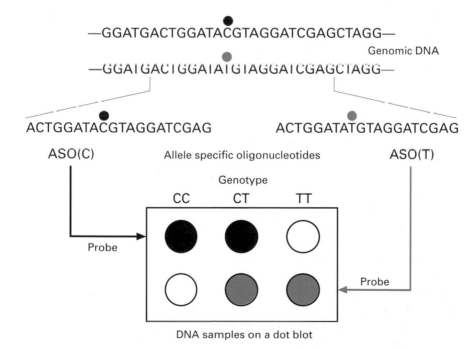

Figure 2.4: Allele-specific oligonucleotide (ASO) dot blot analysis of a cytosine–thymine (C–T) polymorphism.

2.2 The characterization of DNA polymorphism

Now that we have described the individual techniques that are required to generate a DNA fingerprint, we shall discuss how these technical elements are combined to characterize and analyze DNA polymorphism. Two alternative routes may be pursued. One is to aim at one locus at a time, the single-locus approach, whereas the other is to analyze several loci simultaneously, the multilocus approach. The latter method yields a DNA fingerprint in one step; the former gives a multilocus DNA profile only by combining a number of locus-specific assays.

2.2.1 Single-locus approaches to DNA polymorphism

DNA polymorphisms were first studied by analyzing DNA digested with restriction enzymes using Southern blotting and molecular hybridization techniques. An example of such an experiment is illustrated in *Figure 2.5*. In this particular case, genomic DNA from three individuals was digested with the restriction enzyme *Msp*I, gel-separated, blotted on to a

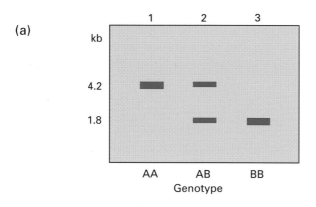

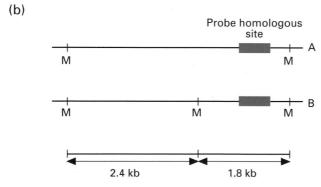

Figure 2.5: A restriction fragment length polymorphism (RFLP). (a) Southern blot experiment with three genomic DNA samples digested with restriction enzyme *Msp*I. The different observed patterns are labeled 1, 2 and 3. (b) Schematic representation of the corresponding chromosomes (A and B). The site of hybridization of the probe is marked. M: *Msp*I restriction site.

membrane, and subsequently hybridized with a radiolabeled DNA probe. Three alternative patterns arose: (1) shows a strong band of 4.2 kb, (3) has a strong band of 1.8 kb, and (2) exhibits both bands, each at about half the intensity of the other two patterns.

The interpretation of this result is easy when it is remembered that humans are diploid organisms – every individual carries two homologous chromosomes in somatic cells, one inherited from the mother and one from the father. Patterns (1) and (3) are due to both chromosomes being identical with respect to the polymorphism revealed here (homozygosity), and band pattern (2) is due to the two chromosomes being different (heterozygosity). *Figure 2.5b* depicts these two chromosomes, abbreviated as A and B, showing that the difference between them is due to the presence of an additional *Msp*I recognition site on chomosome B, and the absence of this site on chromosome A. Thus, pattern (1) corresponds to the presence of two A chromosomes (genotype AA), pattern (3) reflects the presence of two B chromosomes (genotype BB), and pattern (2) is due to the presence of one A and one B chromosome (genotype AB).

The type of polymorphism just described is called a restriction fragment length polymorphism (RFLP), because it obviously comprises restriction fragments of different lengths. The cause of the length difference is sequence variation within the recognition sequence itself. Thus, the polymorphism is a restriction site polymorphism (RSP). This subclassification is necessary because there are other types of RFLPs which are not due to alterations of the restriction enzyme recognition site itself.

Figure 2.6 shows the analysis of genomic DNA from the same three individuals as in *Figure 2.5*, following digestion with the restriction enzymes *Hin*fI and *Hae*III, Southern blotting, and probing with another DNA probe. All three individuals show different patterns, but these appear to be independent of the enzyme used, differing only with respect to the absolute but not the relative size of the bands. *Figure 2.6b* illustrates the molecular basis of this polymorphism. Although the restriction sites themselves are invariant, the space between them is not. The different chromosomes contain different numbers of short, tandemly arranged repetitive sequence elements. This type of polymorphism is called a variable number of tandem repeat (VNTR) polymorphism. Note that a probe has been used that recognizes a unique (i.e. locus-specific) DNA sequence flanking the repeat array.

With PCR technology many RFLPs can be visualized, bypassing the rather laborious method of Southern blotting. A PCR reaction will usually generate enough DNA to be directly visible on a gel after staining. If the PCR-amplified DNA of an RSP-containing region is cut by the corresponding enzyme prior to electrophoresis, band size differences show up directly (*Figure 2.7*). Similarly, a VNTR-containing locus may also be investigated directly using the PCR approach (*Figure 2.8*).

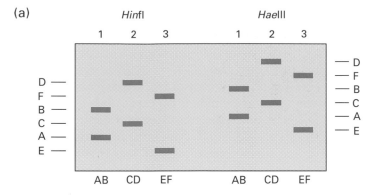

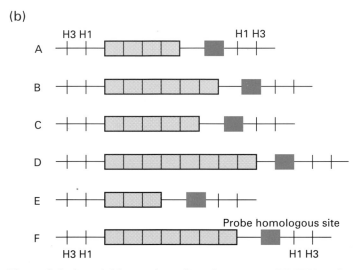

Figure 2.6: A variable number of tandem repeat (VNTR) polymorphism.
(a) Southern blot experiment with the genomic DNA samples 1, 2 and 3 of *Figure 2.5*, digested with *Hin*fI and *Hae*III, respectively. (b) Schematic representation of the corresponding chromosomes (A–F). Boxed area: array of a short, tandemly repeated sequence; H1: *Hin*fI restriction site; H3: *Hae*III restriction site.

So far, we have considered only polymorphisms that manifest themselves in interchromosomal length differences of the DNA segment under study. In order to characterize such polymorphisms precisely, a technique was required by which the DNA fragments could be size-separated. However, when the question is reduced to determining the presence or absence of a particular DNA sequence, then simpler methods, such as the ASO approach (Section 2.1.9), can be used.

There are, of course, many other types of polymorphism than those described above that can be studied at the DNA level. Deletions, insertions and rearrangements of smaller or larger segments occur in the human and other genomes. Outside coding regions, such sequence alterations are usually of no phenotypic consequence, and may thus also

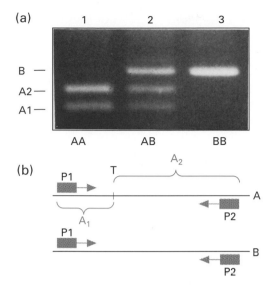

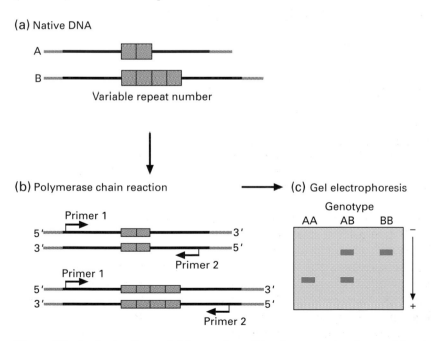

Figure 2.7: Restriction fragment length polymorphism analysis based on PCR. (a) Genomic DNA of three individuals (1–3) was amplified by PCR using primers P1 and P2. PCR products were digested with restriction enzyme *Taq*I and size-fractionated. (b) Schematic representation of the corresponding chromosomes (A and B). T: variable *Taq*I restriction site.

Figure 2.8: Analysis of a variable number of tandem repeat polymorphism by PCR. The length differences caused by variable repeat numbers on different chromosomes (a) is analyzed using PCR primers flanking the polymorphic site (b). PCR end-products are size-separated, yielding a characteristic pattern for each genotype (c).

attain population frequencies high enough to be useful for DNA fingerprinting.

An ever-expanding collection of single-copy probes is available today and is in current use in forensic and medical settings as well as in basic genetic research. In order to obtain DNA profiles of optimal discriminatory power, as required, for example, in most forensic casework, probes have to be combined which:

(1) detect loci not linked to each other and lacking allelic association (see Section 4.1.2);
(2) are specific for a single locus each;
(3) detect polymorphic loci with a sufficient number of alleles of appropriate frequencies (see Section 4.2.2);
(4) create easily interpretable gel or blot patterns (e.g. one band in homozygotes, two bands in heterozygotes).

Wong *et al.* [1] and Smith *et al.* [2] have described a set of five probes which have a calculated probability of less than one in 3×10^{13} of producing identical DNA profiles from two unrelated individuals. *Figure 2.9* shows the results of applying three probes (MS8, MS43 and G3) and two of these probes (MS1 and MS31), respectively, in a small nuclear family with mother, father and child. It should be noted that, in contrast to DNA fingerprints obtained with multilocus probes, these banding patterns are simple superimpositions of complete single-locus patterns.

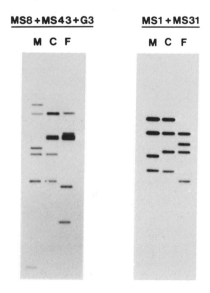

MS8+MS43+G3   **MS1+MS31**

  M C F   M C F

Figure 2.9: DNA profiling in kinship analysis. Southern blot of genomic DNA of a nuclear family, probed with combinations of three (MS8, MS43, G3) and two (MS1, MS31) of single-locus probes, respectively. The child's pattern (C) is a composite of bands also seen in the mother (M) and the father (F). Photograph courtesy of Cellmark Diagnostics, Abingdon, Oxfordshire, UK.

One of the most variable and thus informative loci described to date, D1S7, is among those detected by the aforementioned probes (MS1). It has a 9 bp basic repeat unit. More than 99% of individuals tested so far have been heterozygous, with alleles ranging from 1 kb to 23 kb. Theoretically, more than 2400 different allelic length states can be expected at this locus. Since not all of these can be resolved by conventional agarose gel electrophoresis, quasi-continuous allele length distributions result (see Section 4.2). Zischler *et al.* [3] have recently reported on a set of similarly efficient single-locus probes which were derived from sequences containing $(CAC)_n$ repeat elements (Section 2.2.3).

It has been known for a long time that the constituent repeats of minisatellites are not necessarily completely identical but may differ slightly from the core sequence [4]. It is again thanks to Alec Jeffreys and his co-workers that this observation was systematically exploited by a technique called minisatellite variant repeat mapping by PCR (MVR–PCR), also referred to as 'digital DNA fingerprinting' [5]. The method was established for the minisatellite locus D1S8, detected by probe MS32, which comprises at least 50 different length alleles, with the repeat units measuring 29 bp. Some of the repeat units, however, show base substitutions, and the ordering of wild-type and mutant repeat units within an array defines a huge variety of alleles. Using combinations of PCR primers specific for these sequence variants and primers outside the repeat array common to all alleles, highly individual-specific digital codes can be generated. The great advantage of this approach rests on the fact that phenotype and genotype data are easily computerized. This novel technique is likely to be highly useful both in forensic analyses and in paternity testing.

2.2.2 A quantitative measure of polymorphism

The degree of polymorphism of a DNA system is usually measured by the so-called polymorphism information content (PIC) value [6]. This quantity is used mainly in the context of gene mapping and indirect genetic diagnosis, where it has the following important practical meaning.

If a DNA locus is closely linked to the gene underlying a dominant inherited disorder, then this locus may serve as a marker for the disease. Typing one offspring for the marker, in addition to the normal and the affected parent, often allows the identification of the chromosome carrying the mutant disease-causing allele. The PIC value measures the probability of success of such an undertaking. Diagnosis is not feasible if the affected parent is homozygous for the marker. If the affected parent is heterozygous, the disease-bearing chromosome can always be identified provided that both parents are not of the same heterozygous marker genotype. In the latter situation, the affected chromosome can be identified only in those 50% of cases where the affected child is not also heterozygous. Thus, when $f_{i,j}$ denotes the frequency of marker genotype A_iA_j,

$$PIC = \sum f_{i,j}(1 - 0.5f_{i,j})$$

where summation is over all heterozygous genotypes.

For illustration, let us assume a locus with three alleles with frequencies $f_1 = 0.2$, $f_2 = 0.3$ and $f_3 = 0.5$. Under so-called Hardy–Weinberg conditions (Section 4.1.1), when genotypes are assumed to be formed by random sampling of gametes, the heterozygote frequencies are $f_{i,j} = 2f_if_j$. Thus, $f_{1,2} = 0.12$, $f_{1,3} = 0.20$, and $f_{2,3} = 0.30$. Therefore,

$$PIC = (0.12 \times 0.94) + (0.20 \times 0.90) + (0.30 \times 0.85) = 0.548.$$

This result implies that the marker alleles may help to identify a dominant mutant allele in 54.8% of nuclear families of the type described.

2.2.3 Multilocus approaches to DNA polymorphism

In principle, a multilocus DNA fingerprint can be generated either by the simultaneous application of several probes, each one specific for a particular locus, or by applying a single DNA probe that simultaneously detects several loci. In practice, the latter approach has been adopted but, as will be discussed in Section 5.2, the quantitative analysis of such multilocus patterns has sometimes been seriously misinterpreted as dealing with superimposed single-locus patterns.

In Section 2.2.1, it was noted that a VNTR polymorphism at a specific locus is normally visualized using a DNA probe flanking the polymorphic repeat array. However, if the elements of a repeat array occur not only at that one locus but also recur in other parts of the genome (again in tandem repeats and perhaps also in variable numbers), then the repeat sequence itself could be used as a probe in order to obtain a multilocus pattern. The position and intensity of individual bands in this pattern would depend mainly on two potential variables: (1) the average number of repeat elements covered by an array, and (2) the distance between the repeat array and the nearest recognition site for the restriction enzyme used. The relative contribution of these two variables depends critically upon what proportion of the restriction fragment is actually occupied by the repeat array. If this proportion is large, the band position and intensity will be roughly proportional to the element number of the array. However, if it is small, the element number will influence only band intensity, whereas the band position will depend mainly on sequence characteristics outside the repeat array.

Common sense tells us that the number of loci detected by a multilocus probe must be limited in order to yield patterns that are useful. Too few loci would mean little improvement over the single-locus approach; too many loci might overstrain the resolving power of the electrophoretic systems and result in a smear. Most multilocus systems presently in use represent a compromise. Only a size 'window' of the electrophoretic pattern can actually be interpreted, usually in the 4–20 kb range, whilst the larger number of smaller fragments are poorly resolvable and are therefore disregarded in the analysis. Nevertheless, it is important to remember that DNA fragments derived from distinct loci may coincide even in the resolvable portion of the multilocus pattern (see also Section 4.3).

As with single-locus probes, a large number of multilocus systems have been developed. In contrast to single-locus probes which, by definition, detect a unique locus each, there is considerable overlap between some multilocus probes with respect to the loci with which they react. This means that expanding a set of single-locus probes will always increase the amount of information, whereas the application of several multilocus probes may not. As yet, the molecular basis of this phenomenon is only poorly understood. It is interesting to note that many multilocus probes have been shown to cross-hybridize to polymorphic loci in a wide range of animal and plant species. It is not clear whether this obvious sequence conservation also reflects a shared function.

The most widely used multilocus probes, named 33.6 and 33.15, were developed in the laboratory of Alec Jeffreys, who also coined the term 'DNA fingerprinting' when first describing their properties [7]. These probes typically detect 17 variable DNA fragments per individual in the size range of 3.5–20 kb. Only about 1% of fragments are co-detected by both probes [8]. Other multilocus approaches to human DNA fingerprinting are based on cross-hybridizing probes derived from bacteriophage M13 [9], the α-globin 3′ hypervariable region [10], and the major eggshell protein of *Schistosoma mansonii* [11].

Detailed analyses of 33.6 and 33.15 revealed that, at the genomic level, the minisatellites detected by these probes are composed of tandem arrays of 3–40 elements having a core sequence of GGGCAGGANG (with N standing for any of the four bases). Between different arrays, considerable variation is seen with respect to the extent of sequence heterogeneity among their constituent elements. It was found that probes derived from arrays with high element homogeneity pick up a high degree of repeat number polymorphism in the population, and vice versa. This is the expected result when the polymorphism is generated by unequal crossing-over events during meiosis (see Section 3.2.1).

It also follows from these observations that a further potential factor influencing band intensity may be the degree of homology between the probe and the target sequence. If the repeat elements contain mutations destroying their perfect repetitivity, then the amount of resulting hybrid molecules may vary with the stringency of the experimental conditions.

Another multilocus DNA fingerprinting system that deserves special attention makes use of synthetic oligonucleotides. This approach was devised and developed by Jörg Epplen and his group [12]. Based on the observation that certain simple repeat sequences such as GATA or GACA are common to all eukaryotic genomes [13, 14], probes were constructed that are capable of detecting hypervariable loci and thus can generate DNA fingerprints from human DNA. These probes include multimers of CA, CT, GATA, GACA, GAA, GGAT, or TCC. However, the highest degree of genetic individualization in humans was achieved using a CAC pentamer [15], which is now widely used in paternity testing [16] (*Figure 2.10*). It is difficult to fit the oligonucleotide approach into the framework outlined in *Table 1.4*, because here microsatellite probes generate minisatellite-like patterns. It is as yet unclear how polymorphism at loci detected by probe $(CAC)_5$ actually comes about, but it can be speculated that the observed patterns derive from perfect repeats lying adjacent to more degenerate repeats, thus forming simple minisatellites. An overlap between loci detected by $(CAC)_5$ and those hybridizing to MZ1.3 has been demonstrated [17].

Vergnaud [18] has contributed further to the oligonucleotide approach by polymerizing random oligonucleotides to form synthetic tandem repeat probes. These probes predominantly hybridize to loci also detected by other naturally occurring minisatellites [19].

2.3 Applications in human genome research and clinical medicine

This book is primarily concerned with DNA fingerprinting and DNA profiling in relation to forensic medicine and kinship testing. There are, however, many other fields where this technology has been applied successfully, and these are briefly summarized below.

2.3.1 Mapping the human genome

Linkage analysis aims at identifying genetic signposts pointing towards genes of hitherto unknown localization. Such studies result in estimates of the genetic distance between the unknown gene and a linked marker locus, expressed in recombination units. Two genetic loci are said to be one centi-Morgan (cM) apart if they recombine (Section 1.2.6), on average, in one per 100 meioses. In humans, the goal of detecting close linkage between an unknown gene and a marker can be achieved only by studying large pedigrees or large sets of pairs of close relatives. Since there is often not even a hint as to the chromosomal location of the gene, a large number of (previously mapped) markers must be tested. These should be polymorphic enough to allow recombinant and nonrecombinant meioses to be distinguished, and markers are most efficient when evenly distributed throughout the genome.

Repetitive DNA sequences are among the most informative markers for linkage analysis. In 1980, Botstein and co-workers [6] first outlined the potential use of RFLPs in linkage studies. These authors estimated that about 150 markers, spread out over the human genome at 20 cM intervals,

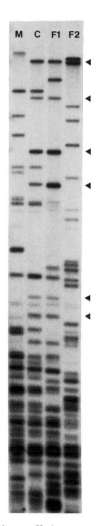

Figure 2.10: DNA fingerprinting with oligonucleotide probe $(CAC)_5$. DNA from mother (M) and child (C) has been analyzed side by side with DNA from two suspected fathers (F1 and F2). Arrowheads indicate nonmaternal offspring bands.

would be sufficient to map any gene responsible for a given phenotypic trait without direct access to its DNA sequence. Twelve years later, in October 1992, *Nature* published an article by Weissenbach *et al.* [20], entitled "A second generation linkage map of the human genome". In this article, the construction of a human linkage map was reported that was based on over 800 newly characterized microsatellites containing $(CA)_n$ repeats. With only one exception where localization failed, all these microsatellites could be assigned to one of the 22 autosomes or the X chromosome. Three out of four exhibited a heterozygosity rate above 0.7, and almost 70% of the markers could be ordered with high reliability (odds ratios above 1000:1). The resulting linkage map was shown to span approximately 90% of the human genome at an average marker density of 5 cM.

Since then, many other linkage maps have been reported based on microsatellite polymorphisms. On chromosome 21, for example, 43 new markers with an average heterozygosity of 0.6 have been reported, which reduce the average spacing of markers on this chromosome to 2.5 cM. Similar progress has been made on the long arm (q) of chromosome 9 using (CA)$_n$-containing microsatellites. With pairwise distances all below 15 cM, 13 new markers were found to cover approximately 90 cM of 9q.

Multilocus DNA fingerprinting also provides a promising source of markers for linkage studies. This is because the loci detected by a multilocus probe are highly polymorphic, and several of them can be analyzed in a single experiment. The disadvantages, however, are: (1) allelism of DNA fingerprint bands in different pedigrees is difficult to determine, and (2) not all potentially resolvable loci can be analyzed in a given pedigree. Furthermore, clustering of some 'fingerprint loci' in particular regions of the genome seriously limits their efficiency in linkage studies.

The genetic complexity of DNA fingerprints is enormous. For probes 33.6 and 33.15, for example, Jeffreys *et al.* [21] found that most of the DNA fingerprint fragments transmitted in two large families could not be paired as alleles. Their findings suggested that the patterns obtained were derived from approximately 60 heterozygous loci, only a proportion of which could be scored in a single individual. When allelic and linked DNA fragments were excluded from consideration, the simultaneous analysis of up to 34 unlinked loci was still possible, and these loci were presumably scattered over most of the human autosomes.

One way of getting around the problems caused by the complex nature of multilocus DNA fingerprints is to clone individual DNA fragments from them. This approach should yield locus-specific probes which, due to the high rate of detected heterozygosity, would be ideal for linkage analysis. Six variable loci detected in human DNA by hybridization with DNA fingerprint probes 33.6 and 33.15 have been characterized by Wong *et al.* [1]. All of the cloned minisatellite probes specifically detect polymorphic Mendelian loci, exhibiting heterozygosity rates from 90% to 99%, and being dispersed over chromosomes 1, 5, 7 and 12. Even where two markers lie on the same chromosome they show no detectable linkage, indicating that they are located far apart on the chromosome. Since there is no clustering of these loci, they should provide valuable markers.

In a similar study, Wells *et al.* [22] followed the segregation of several minisatellite loci through two large human pedigrees. Linkage analysis with previously mapped RFLPs allowed the local assignment of 31 out of 146 minisatellite alleles. However, the results suggested that the corresponding loci cluster at the end points of chromosomes (telomeres; ter). A group of at least five separate minisatellites was found at 7qter in a region of excess male meiotic recombination. This finding is in agreement with the observation of other minisatellite clusters occuring at the end of the short arm of chromosome 16 (16pter) and in the pseudoautosomal region (i.e. that part of the sex chromosomes which is homologous between X and Y). Both these regions are known to represent male recombinational hotspots.

The application of fingerprint-derived single-locus probes to the mapping of human genetic disease was illustrated by Fowler *et al.* [10]. These authors used a probe to produce DNA fingerprints which detects a hypervariable region 3' to the α-globin locus on chromosome 16. Segregation analysis revealed a number of randomly dispersed DNA fragments, inherited in a Mendelian fashion with minimal allelism to each other. Adult polycystic kidney disease was found to be closely linked to the α-globin gene cluster on 16p, using this probe as a marker.

2.3.2 Tumor biology

Whereas normal somatic cells of higher organisms have low mutation rates, and are thus genetically stable, tumor cells are characterized by dramatically more frequent genetic changes. Structural and numerical chromosome alterations are often seen, some of which are nonspecific and secondary to tumorigenesis, whereas others are causative. Because minisatellite loci are dispersed over the entire chromosome complement, the chromosomal rearrangements taking place in tumor tissues are usually associated with alterations of the DNA fingerprint pattern and can be revealed, for example, by suitable multilocus probes. Compared to patterns obtained from normal tissues of the same individual, tumor DNA fingerprints should reveal loss, gain or intensity alterations of bands (for a recent review, see Ref. 23).

Gliomas (which account for the vast majority of primary tumors of the central nervous system in humans), for example, are known to be associated with a multitude of different numerical and structural chromosome abnormalities. Nürnberg *et al.* [24] have shown that these nonspecific chromosome alterations are paralleled by similarly nonspecific changes of the $(CAC)_5$ banding pattern. However, from a subset of five out of 31 gliomas, each exhibited a highly amplified tumor-specific (but not individual-specific) band of identical size. This band was associated in all cases with a dramatic amplification of the epidermal growth factor receptor gene, an oncogene implicated in tumorigenesis. Thus, DNA fingerprinting appears to be a sound alternative to conventional cytogenetic tumor monitoring, especially since the latter is often a tedious exercise and sometimes highly inefficient. Furthermore, it has become apparent that DNA fingerprinting may even provide clues as to the molecular etiology of cancer.

Other applications of DNA fingerprinting in clinical oncology include the study of tumor clonality, discrimination between metastatic disease and primary tumor multiplicity, assessment of viral etiology, and monitoring therapy and residual disease.

2.3.3 Transplantation medicine

Transplantation medicine is another field in which DNA fingerprinting has been used clinically (e.g. see Ref. 25). When DNA fingerprinting is performed in patients and donors before and after bone marrow transplantation, it is possible to evaluate engraftment. This approach is especially useful when patient and donor are HLA-identical, of the same sex, and have the same ABO-Rhesus blood type. Thus, it has been possible to study short- and long-term results, covering relapse and remission stages, in a variety of clinical settings including therapy of leukemia or aplastic anemia states. Similarly, the fate of keratinocyte transplants used as allografts on burn wounds has been followed [27].

2.3.4 Medical microbiology

Apart from forensic medicine and kinship testing, it is probably in medical microbiology and parasitology that DNA fingerprinting has borne the richest fruit as a diagnostic tool (e.g. see Ref. 26). Clinical epidemiology of viral, bacterial and parasitic disease requires quick and informative test systems for the study of strain differentiation, the study of isolates as well as the tracing of source, transmission and spread of disease outbreaks, all of which are measures on which the control of epidemics and treatment of patients strongly rely. For example, DNA fingerprinting allows identification of human DNA present in blood meals of hematophagous arthropods, providing epidemiologically useful information relevant to the control of arthropod-borne microbial and parasitic disease [28]. Depending on the genome size of the organism under study and on probe availability, either classical Southern-blot-type DNA fingerprints (with specific markers such as ribosomal DNA) or pulsed-field gel electrophoresis have been used in such experiments. The latter method allows discrimination and mapping of large, megabase-sized molecules.

2.4 References

1. Wong, Z., Wilson, V., Patel, I., Povey, S. and Jeffreys, A.J. (1987) *Ann. Hum. Genet.,* **51,** 269.
2. Smith, J.C., Anwar, R., Riley, J. *et al.* (1990) *J. Forens. Sci. Soc.,* **30,** 19.
3. Zischler, H., Kammerbauer, C., Studer, R., Grzeschik, K.H. and Epplen, J.T. (1992) *Genomics,* **13,** 983.
4. Owerbach, D. and Aagaard, L. (1984) *Gene,* **32,** 475.
5. Jeffreys, A.J., McLeod, A., Tamaki, K., Neil, D.L. and Monckton, D.G. (1991) *Nature,* **354,** 204.
6. Botstein, D., White, R.L., Skolnick, M. and Davis, R.W. (1980) *Am. J. Hum. Genet.,* **32,** 314.
7. Jeffreys, A.J., Wilson, V. and Thein, L.S. (1985) *Nature,* **314,** 67.
8. Jeffreys, A.J., Turner, M. and Debenham, P. (1991) *Am. J. Hum. Genet.,* **48,** 824.

9. Vassart, G., Georges, M., Monsieur, R., Brocas, H., Lequarre, A.S. and Christophe, D. (1987) *Science,* **235,** 683.
10. Fowler, S.J., Gill, P., Werret, D.J. and Higgs, D.R. (1988) *Hum. Genet.,* **79,** 142.
11. Pena, S.D.J., Macedo, A.M., Braga, V.M.M. *et al.* (1990) *Nucl. Acids Res.,* **18,** 7466
12. Ali, S., Müller, C.R. and Epplen, J.T. (1986) *Hum. Genet.,* **74,** 239.
13. Singh, L., Purdom, I.F. and Jones, K.W. (1981) *Cold Spring Harbor Symp. Quant. Biol.,* **45,** 805.
14. Epplen, J.T., McCarrey, J.R., Sutou, S. *et al.* (1982) *Proc. Natl Acad. Sci. USA,* **79,** 3798.
15. Schäfer, R., Zischler, H., Birsner, U., Becker, A. and Epplen, J.T. (1988) *Electrophoresis,* **9,** 369.
16. Krawczak, M., Böhm, I., Nürnberg, P. *et al.* (1993) *Forens. Sci. Int.,* **59,** 101.
17. Luckenbach, C., Rodewyk, S. and Ritter, H. (1991) *Int. J. Legal Med.,* **104,** 303.
18. Vergnaud, G. (1989) *Nucl. Acids Res.,* **17,** 7623.
19. Armour, J.A.L., Vergnaud, G. and Crosier, M. (1992) *Hum. Mol. Genet.,* **1,** 319.
20. Weissenbach, J., Gyapay, G., Dib, C., Vignal, A., Morisette, J., Millasseau, P., Vaysseix, G. and Lathrop, M. (1992) *Nature,* **359,** 794.
21. Jeffreys, A.J., Wilson, V., Thein, L.S., Weatherall, D.J. and Ponder, B.A.J. (1986) A*m. J. Hum. Genet.,* **39,** 11.
22. Wells, R.A., Green, P. and Reeders, S.T, (1989) *Genomics,* **5,** 761.
23. Matsumura, Y. and Tarin, D. (1992) *Cancer Res.,* **52,** 2174.
24. Nürnberg, P., Zischler, H., Fuhrmann, E., Thiel, G., Losanova, T., Kinzel, D., Nisch, G., Witkowski, R. and Epplen, J.T. (1991) *Genes Chromosom. Cancer,* **3,** 79.
25. Pakkala, S. (1992) *Int. J. Clin. Lab. Res.,* **21,** 269.
26. Römling, U., Grothues, D., Heuer, T. *et al.* (1992) *Electrophoresis,* **13,** 626.
27. Van der Merwe, A.E., Mattheyse, F.J., Bedford, M., van Helden, P.D. and Rossouw, D.J. (1990) *Burns,* **16,** 193.
28. Coulson, R.M., Curtis, C.F., Ready, P.D., Hill, N. and Smith, D.F. (1990) *Med. Vet. Entomol.,* **4,** 357.

Further reading

Burke, T., Dolf, G., Jeffreys, A.J. and Wolff, R. (1991) *DNA Fingerprinting: Approaches and Applications.* Birkhäuser Verlag, Basel.

Cooper, D.N. and Krawczak, M. (1993) *Human Gene Mutation.* BIOS Scientific Publishers, Oxford.

Epplen, J.T. (1992) in *Advances in Electrophoresis* (A. Chrambach, M.J. Dunn and B.J. Radola, eds), VCH, Weinheim, p. 59.

Newton, C.R. and Graham, A. (1994) *PCR.* BIOS Scientific Publishers, Oxford.

Pena, S.D.J., Chakraborty, R., Epplen, J.T. and Jeffreys, A.J. (1993) *DNA Fingerprinting: State of the Science.* Birkhäuser Verlag, Basel.

Strachan, T. (1992) *The Human Genome.* BIOS Scientific Publishers, Oxford.

Chapter 3

Origin and maintenance of DNA polymorphism

3.1 The principles of molecular evolution

The diversity exhibited by human DNA is the result of a long-lasting interaction between the creative power of mutation and the maintaining and destructive forces of selection and chance. Precisely how genetic characteristics have evolved over time is indeed one of the most enigmatic aspects of human history – and a controversial one too. A scientific debate has raged for decades over the question as to whether most of our genetic make-up has been determined by natural selection, favoring beneficial alleles over disadvantageous mutations and eliminating the latter from the gene pool, or whether the majority of *de novo* mutations have been (almost) neutral and have accumulated due to genetic drift (i.e. the stochastic fluctuation of gene frequencies in small, ancient populations). A comprehensive description of the theory of molecular evolution is well beyond the scope of this book. However, some basic principles are essential for an understanding of the molecular characteristics that allow inferences to be made about identity and relatedness by genetic means. These principles will be reviewed briefly in the following sections.

3.1.1 Mutation

The term 'mutation' denotes both the process and the result of changes in the genetic material. As far as evolution is concerned, only inherited mutations are relevant. Only these are able to survive in time, to accumulate, and ultimately to determine the genetic characteristics of individuals, populations or species.

In diploid species such as humans, the chance of survival of an individual mutation is small. If inbreeding is neglected and if the population under study is sufficiently large, every new mutation will show up exclusively in heterozygotes, and only half of their descendants will inherit the mutation. This implies that, among k offspring of a mutation carrier, the chance of extinction of that mutation (i.e. nontransmission in all k meioses) is $\frac{1}{2}^k$. The fate of a single mutation in a large population is illustrated in *Figure 3.1*, assuming that the number of offspring per individual follows a Poisson distribution, and that the average number of offspring is two (i.e. that the population size is constant). Given that the mutation is neutral, which means that it has neither advantageous nor disadvantageous phenotypic effects, it can be calculated that approximately 85% of mutant alleles will survive for no longer than 10 generations. The probability of extinction is unity. Although a small number of mutations may manage to persist in the gene pool for a long period of time (*Figure 3.1*), all of them share the same ultimate fate of disappearance.

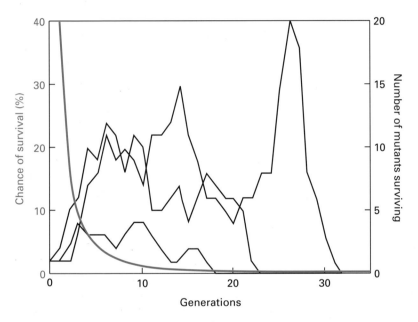

Generations

Figure 3.1: The fate of single mutations in large outbred populations without selection. Orange line: average chance of a single mutation surviving at least the given number of generations. Black lines: number of mutations remaining after the given number of generations. Three simulated cases characterized by a comparatively long persistence are shown.

One way for a given type of mutation to reach a significant population frequency would be if the losses were compensated for by fresh mutations. On the other hand, if mutation occurs in germ cells at a fixed rate, this mutational 'pressure' would result in an ultimate ousting of the wild-type by the mutant alleles. This displacement could be averted by backward mutation. In order to illustrate this interplay, consider the simple situation of two different alleles at a single locus, A_1 and A_2, which undergo mutation at rates μ_1 (A_1 to A_2) and μ_2 (A_2 to A_1), respectively. If p_i denotes the population frequency of allele A_i ($p_1 + p_2 = 1$), then the proportion of lost copies of A_1 is $p_1 \cdot \mu_1$ per generation, whereas the increase in frequency amounts to $p_2 \cdot \mu_2$. For these two to balance out, the relation

$$p_1 \cdot \mu_1 = p_2 \cdot \mu_2$$

that is

$$p_1/p_2 = \mu_2/\mu_1$$

has to hold. Thus, the allele frequencies will approach an equilibrium state in which their relative ratio equals that of the mutation rates towards the corresponding allele.

In reality, however, such equilibrium frequencies are rarely observed. With a variety of RFLPs in humans, for example, alleles defined by the presence of a restriction site are more common than alleles corresponding to its absence (see Section 2.2.1). It is intuitively obvious that mutations resulting in the loss of restriction sites are much more likely than mutations creating or restoring them (a restriction site is a specific string of nucleotides; most changes within it will destroy the site, but only a specific change will create or restore a site). In conclusion, *de novo* mutation appears to represent only the source of blanks for the 'evolutionary workshop', and other mechanisms need to be invoked in order to explain how genetic diversity is actually maintained.

3.1.2 Gene flow

Complete isolation of human populations occurs only rarely; at least a minimum of migration has taken place between most spatially and culturally separated groups in human history. Whenever mating took place in such situations between local and immigrant partners, genes from the outside world were transmitted to the progeny, which therefore represented a genetic mixture of two formerly distinct entities. This process of *gene flow* is a very efficient and rapid way of changing the genetic structure of populations. When novel alleles are originally rare, gene flow increases their relative frequency in the invaded population. The smaller the original population is, and the more numerous the invaders are, the more pronounced this effect will be.

A very recent example of gene flow is provided by the black and white populations of North America. For certain genes determining blood groups, comparison of the allele frequencies between West Africa and the US revealed that US Black populations living in larger cities have received as much as 25% of their genes from the Caucasoid gene pool. This process has required less than 300 years (i.e. ten generations).

3.1.3 Selection

Up to now it has been assumed that all individuals within a population have the same chance of contributing their genes to future generations, irrespective of their genotype. However, many inherited conditions in humans reduce the ability to reproduce. Depending on whether the mutant gene function is dominant or recessive, the link between genotype and phenotype allows only a portion of disadvantageous mutations to slip into the genetic heritage. Thus, there is *selection* against some genotypes.

In population genetics, reproductive ability is measured by the number of offspring. This parameter (f_{ij}) is called the reproductive (or biological) fitness of genotype A_iA_j and is usually expressed relative to one particular genotype, such as the heterozygote A_1A_2. Often, the so-called coefficient of selection (s_{ij}), which equals $1-f_{ij}$, is used instead of the fitness. Parameter s_{ij} is a measure of the reproductive disadvantage that individuals with genotype A_iA_j experience in comparison to the heterozygote A_1A_2. For example, if a homozygote A_1A_1 has on average 10% fewer offspring than a heterozygote A_1A_2, then his or her relative fitness, f_{11}, is 0.9 and the coefficient of selection, s_{11}, is 0.1.

It can be shown that the equilibrium allele frequencies, at which the opposing forces of selection against (or in favor of) the two homozygous genotypes A_1A_1 and A_2A_2 are balanced, are given by

$$p_1/p_2 = s_{22}/s_{11}.$$

This means that each equilibrium allele frequency is proportional to the coefficient of selection against the opposite homozygous genotype. If selection against A_2A_2 is small, allele A_1 will be rare, and vice versa.

As far as stability of the selection equilibrium is concerned, three situtations must be distinguished. If $s_{11} > 0$ and $s_{22} > 0$, which means that there is heterozygote advantage, then the equilibrium is stable and any distortion due to exogenous causes is compensated for by selection. If $s_{11} = 0$ and $s_{22} = 0$, there is no selection. In this case, the equilibrium is indifferent, and other indifferent equilibria are adopted when the allele frequencies change due to mutation or migration. Finally, $s_{11} < 0$ and $s_{22} < 0$ means that there is heterozygote disadvantage. Selection patterns like this will result in instability and the ultimate fixation of either A_1 or A_2.

A well-known example of a polymorphism due to heterozygote advantage is that of the sickle cell allele, HbS. Homozygotes for this particular allele of the human β-globin gene suffer from severe anemia and usually die before they reach reproductive age. Nevertheless, one in 500 newborn US Blacks has sickle cell anemia. In Africa, where the incidence is as high as one in 25 newborns in some places, the disease occurs most often in regions where malaria has been frequent in the past. Heterozygotes for HbS are more resistant than normal homozygotes to infection, probably because infected red blood cells are more efficiently eliminated from their blood circulation. This selective advantage may have compensated for the almost complete selection against homozygous carriers of HbS, thereby allowing the mutant allele to attain its current high frequency.

In principle, different parts of the genome should evolve according to their own individual patterns of selection. However, in reality there is interaction (epistasis) and linkage between loci which implies that selection acting on one locus may influence the allele frequencies at another. Epistatic effects can be illustrated by the simple case of two loci with two alleles each, say, A_1, A_2 and B_1, B_2, respectively. It is assumed in this example that A_1, A_2 and B_1 are neutral, whereas B_2 is a dominant lethal allele. In the absence of interaction, B_2 would be eliminated rapidly by selection while the frequencies of A_1 and A_2 would remain unchanged. However, if allele A_1 is able to mask B_2, which means that gametes containing A_1B_2 chromosomes manage to evade selection, in contrast to A_2B_2 gametes, then A_2 becomes equivalent to B_2 with respect to selection. Either A_1 or B_1, depending on which of the two is more frequent, will ultimately supersede its allelic counterpart A_2 or B_2. This implies that the lethal B_2 allele may well persist in a population at considerable frequency just because a particular allele of an interacting locus has been selected for.

Even if A_1 and A_2 did not convey any physiological consequence, they could nevertheless be subject to selection because of linkage and allelic association (see Section 4.1.2). For example, if the lethal B_2 allele is found considerably more often on chromosomes bearing A_2 than expected by chance alone, the latter will also be eliminated from the gene pool and decrease in frequency. The closer the linkage, the smaller the chance of recombination which, by creation of A_1B_2 haplotypes, would be able to smooth this effect. This phenomenon, called the 'hitch-hiker effect', implies that much of the non-functional DNA in the vicinity of genes or gene-related sequences may be dragged into the selectional mess because of its 'unfavorable' neighborhood. This is especially important for the apparently neutral polymorphisms that contribute to DNA fingerprints and profiles. With only a few exceptions (Section 6.2), repetitive DNA has not yet been found to be directly related to phenotypic variability.

3.1.4 Genetic drift

Genetic drift is defined as the dispersive, random change of allele frequencies. In large populations without mutation, migration and selection, random mating is equivalent to random sampling of gametes, and it is intuitively apparent that allele frequencies must remain constant over successive generations in such populations. In fact, if p_1 denotes the starting frequency of allele A_1, the number of A_1 alleles present in N germ cells drawn at random from the population has mean p_1, independent of N, and variance $p_1 \cdot (1-p_1) \cdot N^{-1}$. Thus, the variance decreases when population size increases, and allele frequencies are less stable over generations in small as compared to large populations.

The instability of allele frequencies can be best illustrated by simulation (*Figure 3.2*). Even for a relatively large, constant number of offspring per generation and a starting value of $p_1 = 0.5$, allele frequencies vary dramatically over the generations. However, the most intriguing observation is that one of the two alleles is always eliminated in finite time. Therefore, a novel mutation has the highest chance of survival and fixation by chance when it turns up in a small, but rapidly expanding population. Which allele survives, in general, depends on its initial frequency.

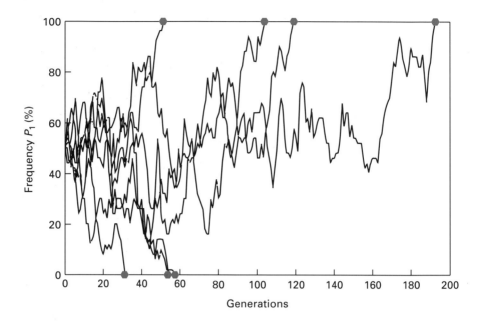

Figure 3.2: Simulations illustrating genetic drift, that is, random frequency fluctuation and ultimate fixation of alleles in small populations. Each generation comprises 50 alleles, representing the descendants of 50 alleles drawn at random from the progenitor gene pool (where p_1, the starting frequency of allele A_1, was 50%).

Such an enrichment of rare alleles has occurred often in human history, including very recently. Several groups of emigrants carried disadvantageous mutations with them on their way to the New World, and some of their progeny still suffer from the high incidence of diseases that are rare elsewhere. One example of this so-called founder effect is provided by the autosomal recessive Ellis-van-Creveld syndrome. The mutation causing this disorder, characterized by inborn heart disease, small stature and morphological anomalies, has attained a frequency of 7% among the Amish people of Pennsylvania, but is very rare everywhere else.

3.1.5 *The selectionist–neutralist controversy*

The phenomenon of genetic drift forms the argumentative basis of the neutral theory of evolution, according to which the majority of the molecular difference between species is due to random fixation of selectively neutral mutations under permanent mutational pressure. The same mechanism has also been invoked to explain intraspecies diversity. Thus, neutral theory regards molecular evolution as an ongoing process, with most of the currently existing polymorphisms and interspecies differences representing only transient states. This view runs contrary to that of neo-Darwinian theory, which proposes that the accumulation and maintenance of mutations is due mainly to the action of positive selection at various evolutionary levels.

The principal difference between these two theories is the inevitable adoption of different evolutionary time scales. Since selection acts on individuals, its unit must be generation number. Neo-Darwinian theory would therefore predict that species with short generation times evolve faster than others. In neutral theory, however, mutational pressure plays the predominant role. As we shall see later in this chapter, many mutational mechanisms are concerned with errors in DNA replication and repair. The impact of these processes is determined by the number of divisions that a germ cell undergoes, and is thus clearly dependent on time. Neutral theory would thus predict equal rates of molecular evolution even in species with different generation times, provided their mechanisms of germ cell development exhibit similar physiological properties.

Since, in terms of evolution, lack of function is equivalent to lack of selection, functionless DNA should evolve more freely than functional parts of the genome and therefore change much faster. However, selectionists would maintain that functionless DNA is not necessarily neutral, because selection operates on whole chromosomal regions. If a nonfunctional mutation arises, just by chance, in close proximity to an advantageous allele of an important gene, its descendants will share the selective advantage of that allele until recombination moves a minority of them on to chromosomes with different genetic backgrounds (haplotypes).

Nevertheless, the level of sequence diversity observed in non-functional DNA is usually much higher than that seen in regions of functional importance, and techniques for DNA fingerprinting and profiling rely heavily upon this. For example, in the mammalian β-globin genes, exon sequences are more similiar to one another than are some noncoding DNA homologs in humans. Further, even within exons of the same gene, nucleotides at which a mutation does not alter the identity of the amino acid are polymorphic more often than others. These molecular genetic findings strongly support the neutral theory of evolution.

Promoters of neutral theory also claim that evolution at the phenotype level, and thus in functionally important regions of the genome, has resulted mainly from random processes [1]. In their view, macro-evolution takes place only when new ecological compartments become available. This liberation from selective constraints allows neutral variants to arise. When some of them turn out to be beneficial in the new environment, the process leads to the adaptive evolution of sometimes completely new taxonomic groups that occupy the compartment. The 'evolutionary outburst' in the early Cambrian period, when multicellular organisms first appeared, may represent an example of this phenomenon.

3.2 Mutational mechanisms contributing to genetic diversity

The jury are still out in the debate between selectionists and neutralists over DNA of physiological importance (e.g. protein-coding regions and regulatory sequences), but the neutralist view is probably correct for the bulk of the human genome which, according to current knowledge, has no obvious biological function (see Section 1.3).

Genetic differences in regions of little or no functional importance are likely to reflect almost exclusively the spectrum of mutational changes underlying them. Therefore, the nature of these variants provides evidence for the molecular mechanisms involved in their creation. In principle, both exogenous and endogenous processes can result in mutation and contribute to genetic diversity. However, since we are mostly interested in constitutive polymorphisms here (i.e. stable genotype patterns that are found identically in all cells of the body), we can restrict our considerations to inherited mutations.

Inherited mutations must have arisen in cells of the germ line and, as far as physiologically relevant mutations are concerned, such lesions are known to be caused mainly by endogenous processes [2]. The contribution of exogenous mutagens to inherited conditions is small, not only because of selection eliminating gross aberrations but also because germ cells, in contrast to most somatic cells, are usually well protected against the negative influence of the outside world. If this argument is extrapolated to the whole genome, we may thus focus our interest on endogenous mutation mechanisms as the major source of genetic diversity in humans.

3.2.1 Duplication

A basic mechanism thought to have driven the molecular evolution of higher genomes is the duplication of genetic material. Duplication events may involve small stretches of DNA (e.g. the size of a gene) as well as entire chromosomal segments, whole chromosomes or even sets of chromosomes. After a (viable) duplication has taken place, the two copies usually evolve independently, accumulating different mutations at different times. In the case of a functional region, one copy may escape selectional pressure and become a pseudogene. In other instances, the two copies may aquire different biological functions.

On the gene scale, a good example of this phenomenon is provided by the human globin genes which cluster in regions of 30 and 50 kb on two different chromosomes (*Figure 3.3*). The α-globin genes exist as two tandemly arranged genes, HBA1 and HBA2, which encode identical amino acid chains. They are located on chromosome 16, together with the ζ-globin gene, HBZ. The HBA1 and HBA2 genes are separated by only 3 kb and show 64% homology to HBZ. About 4 kb upstream of the α-globin gene pair, a second doublet occurs that is strikingly similar to the first. These two sequences ($\psi\alpha_1$ and $\psi\alpha_2$) are in fact functionless pseudo-genes that probably represent a duplication of the HBA1/HBA2 pair. On the short arm of chromosome 11, HBB and HBD, encoding β- and δ-globin respectively, show 93% sequence homology to one another, and they are thought to have emerged from a common ancestor approximately 40 million years ago [3]. The two highly (over 99%) homologous γ-globin encoding genes, HBG1 and HBG2, are located approximately 15 kb upstream of HBB and HBD and have also resulted from a duplication. They are 71% homologous to the HBB/HBD pair. Finally, it appears likely that all human globin genes share a common ancestor from which various lines have split approximately 450 million years ago, at the dawn of vertebrate evolution.

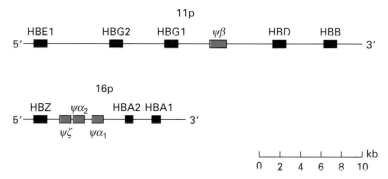

Figure 3.3: Molecular organization of the human globin genes on chromosomes 11 and 16. Functional genes are depicted in black, whereas orange boxes represent pseudogenes.

In principle, the duplication of genetic material can arise by two different mechanisms: recombination and transposition. Recombination, as the name suggests, involves the reciprocal exchange of chromosomal material. As a source of germline mutations, this process of breakage and reunion takes place mainly during the first meiotic division, when DNA replication has almost finished and chromosomes exist as doublets of chromatids (Section 1.2.6). At that time, chromatids line up at regions of high homology, although it is not yet understood how this can be brought about for double-stranded DNA. Recombination can affect both sister chromatids (from the same chromosome) and nonsister chromatids (from different chromosomes).

A prerequisite for recombination resulting in the duplication of genetic material is that a so-called *unequal* crossing-over takes place, which means that cleavage and reunion of the two strands involved does not occur at allelic sites (*Figure 3.4*). As a result, a DNA sequence lying adjacent to the

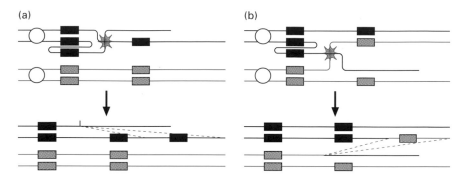

Figure 3.4: Unequal recombination resulting from crossing-over at nonallelic sites of sister (a) or nonsister (b) chromatids (in this case of homologous chromosomes).

nonidentical breakpoints will be found in duplicate on one recombinant chromatid but will be lacking from the other.

Unequal recombination requires the alignment of nonallelic stretches of DNA. Such alignments are normally mediated by sequence homology; so-called illegitimate recombination at sites of minimal or no homology happens only very rarely. This requirement for sequence homology implies that repetitive DNA should be a prime target for unequal recombination. The more alternative sites of alignment that are present, the greater potential there is for sequence variation to be created by duplication. Unequal crossing-over is capable of creating tandem duplications, so this mechanism would explain the existence of VNTR polymorphisms. As outlined in more detail in Section 2.2.1, these polymorphisms consist of constant core motifs that are tandemly arranged in arrays of variable size, and the arrays themselves are spread out in large numbers over the whole genome. When chromatids are brought together at two VNTRs sharing the same core motif, many alternative alignments are possible, and the amount of DNA exchanged in any recombination event can range from a single repeat to entire arrays of them. Nevertheless, as we shall see in Section 3.3, unequal crossing-over does not seem to be the major mechanism generating VNTRs, although it is tempting to believe that this is the case.

Another mechanism of duplication is DNA transposition, and the majority of such events are known to involve RNA intermediates (retro-transposition). Retrotransposition depends critically upon the presence of a special cellular enzyme, reverse transcriptase, which allows RNA to be reverse-transcribed into so-called complementary DNA (cDNA; *Figure 3.5*). When this reverse-transcribed cDNA is integrated into the genome, it exists from then on as an integral copy of the genomic DNA. Since cDNA is complementary to mature RNA, it lacks the exon–intron structure of genomic coding sequences (Section 1.3.2). Indeed, the detection of DNA copies of functional genes without introns has been a milestone in the detection and demonstration of retrotransposition.

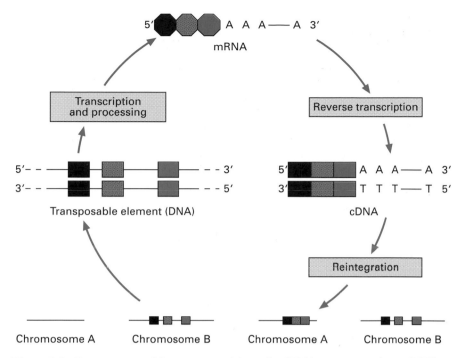

Figure 3.5: Retrotransposition: transposition of a DNA sequence via an RNA intermediate. A DNA sequence on chromosome B is transcribed and processed in mature mRNA, possibly lacking some of the original sequence information. In the presence of the enzyme reverse transcriptase, mRNA can be re-transcribed into DNA which in turn may be capable of integration into another chromosome A.

In addition to protein-coding DNA sequences, retrotransposition also affects a very special class of repetitive DNA that makes up 10–30% of mammalian genomes, the LINE-1 family (see Section 1.3.4). The precise function of the LINE-1 elements, which are up to 7 kb in length, is still unknown even though some large examples contain two highly conserved open reading frames (ORFs). ORFs are pieces of DNA with sequences suggesting they have a protein-coding function. One of the LINE-1-associated ORFs shows homology to a gene encoding a retroviral reverse transcriptase; indeed, a cloned human LINE-1 element expressed *in vitro* in yeast has been shown to have reverse transcriptase activity [2]. It has been suggested that integration of LINE-1 elements is part of the cellular repair mechanism, serving to patch double-stranded breaks in chromosomes. Addition of oligo(T) at the break would create homology to the poly(A)-tail possessed by all LINE-1 elements, and sufficient homology to any region within an element would permit attachment to the other end of the break and subsequent integration involving variable 5′ truncation [4].

A second class of repetitive DNA thought to represent retrotransposons is that of Alu elements, named after an internal cleavage site for restriction endonuclease *Alu*I which is common to all members of this sequence family. Alu elements are approximately 300 bp in size and make up 5% of the human genome. These sequences have been suggested to originate from special RNA species that have been re-integrated at a rate of approximately one integration event per 10 000 years.

3.2.2 Slipped strand mispairing

During replication, DNA becomes single-stranded, and each of the two original strands serves as a template for the polymerization of its complement. During this process the cell is particularly vulnerable to the introduction of mutations, via the temporary dislocation of single-stranded DNA and the subsequent miscorrection of the intermediate constructs by cellular repair mechanisms. Slipped mispairing can cause various types of mutation, including deletions, insertions and single base-pair substitutions. Because of the limited size of the replication fork (less than 300 bp), however, this mechanism is likely to be responsible for only comparatively small aberrations.

Most slipped mispairing events *in vivo* appear to be mediated by direct repeats [2]. In single-stranded conformation, short repetitive sequence motifs may allow one strand of DNA to fold back and to anneal temporarily to the second native strand (*Figure 3.6*). At the site of annealing, one repeat copy plus the sequence lying between the two copies will loop out, forming a target for the cellular DNA repair enzymes. After excision of all or part of the loop, one DNA strand carries a deletion that will be fixed by the subsequent completion of replication synthesis. Alternatively, a nick may be introduced into the unlooped strand opposite the loop. When the resulting gap is filled by polymerase activity, this results in the insertion of genetic material from one repeat copy plus some flanking sequence.

Slippage and dislocated hybridization can also occur between a nascent and a native strand. The possible consequences of this process are the same as just described, although the double-stranded intermediate may be further stabilized by resumed DNA synthesis. For an insertion to take place, no enzyme activity needs to be invoked. When a double-stranded sequence carrying a loop manages to survive, stable elongation would result after the next replication round. In both cases, mismatches resulting from a less than perfect complementarity at the hybridization site can also cause the removal and (templated) miscorrection of single nucleotides (*Figure 3.7*).

Finally, a single-stranded segment may fold back and hybridize to itself, a process that is mediated by palindromic or quasi-palindromic sequences. A palindrome is a pair of complementary DNA sequence motifs either abutting on to each other or separated by a small number of nucleotides such that, when read in a 5′ to 3′ direction, the sequence in each of the two complementary strands is identical. The recognition sites of almost all restriction enzymes are palindromic (e.g. CTGCAG for *Pst*I or GCCNNNNNGGC for *Bgl*I, where N stands for any base). Self-

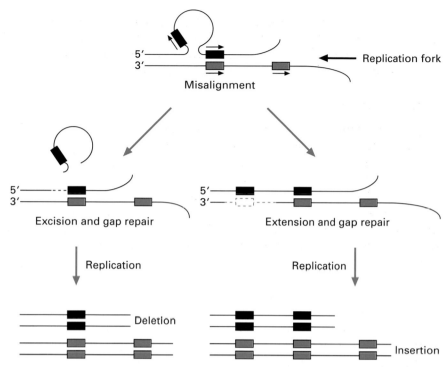

Figure 3.6: Direct repeat-mediated misalignment of native DNA strands during replication. After replication has been completed, the result is either a deletion or an insertion of one repeat copy plus the intervening sequence.

complementarity results in the formation of aberrant hairpin-like structures (*Figure 3.8*). These structures are also targets for cellular DNA repair enzymes. When the self-complementarity is less than perfect, loops, nicks and mismatches are 'corrected', introducing mutations at the corresponding sites. In some instances, all or part of the hairpin structure may be removed.

3.2.3 Errors in DNA replication and repair

DNA replication is a multistep process, and its final accuracy depends on both the fidelity of polymerization and the efficiency of subsequent error correction. Five eukaryotic polymerases are known to exist and to be involved in this process. DNA polymerase α is the major replicative enzyme of the nuclear genome. It binds to large gaps and introduces about 10 bases per association event. Polymerase β is also involved in replication, and has a major function in repair. It is able to fill small nicks, one base at a time. Finally, nuclear DNA is also the substrate of polymerases δ and ε, while polymerase γ is responsible for replication of the mitochondrial genome.

The substitution error rates exhibited *in vitro* vary dramatically between different polymerases and also between different types of substitutions [5]. Polymerase β, for example, is 10 times more prone to making

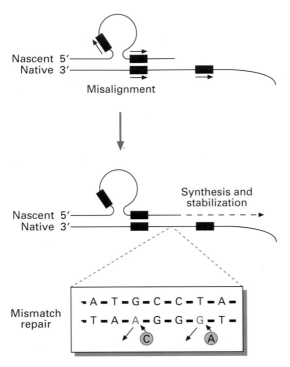

Nascent 5'
Native 3'

Misalignment

Synthesis and
stabilization

Nascent 5'
Native 3'

Mismatch
repair

Figure 3.7: Direct repeat-mediated misalignment of native and nascent DNA strand. As shown, DNA synthesis serves to stabilize the aberrant construct further. After the next replication round, insertion and/or point mutations due to templated miscorrections result.

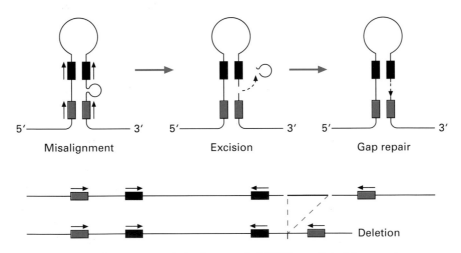

Misalignment   Excision   Gap repair

Deletion

Figure 3.8: Loop structure of single-stranded DNA mediated by quasi-palindromic sequences, and a deletion that may result from 'correction' at this site.

errors than polymerase α, which in turn generates errors 30 times more frequently than polymerase γ. Whereas G is substituted for A by human polymerase α only once in 40 000 insertions, the same enzyme substitutes

C for G at a rate of one in 2500. Local imbalances in the nucleoside pool may either increase or obscure such biases. Nevertheless, each polymerase can be assumed to contribute very specifically to the spectrum of point mutations *in vivo*. For base substitutions in human genes causing inherited disease, the error rates associated with polymerase β were shown to correlate with the observed mutational spectrum [2].

The eukaryotic polymerases exhibit error rates *in vitro* of 10^{-4}–10^{-6} per inserted base, which implies that the high fidelity of DNA replication *in vivo* (10^{-9}–10^{-11} errors per nucleotide replicated) must be the result of a system of post-replicative proofreading and mismatch repair. This repair mechanism, however, is biased and sequence-dependent. G:T mismatches, for example, are repaired very efficiently, but are most often corrected in favor of T to C rather than G to A [6]. Further, the efficiency of repair appears to be somewhat lower in G + C-rich regions of double-stranded DNA.

3.2.4 Chemical DNA modification

Many point mutations are known to result from endogenous enzymatic DNA modification. In eukaryotes, 5-methylcytosine (5mC) is the commonest form of DNA modification and is found almost exclusively adjacent to 3′ flanking G bases. Since 5mC is highly sensitive to spontaneous deamination to thymine (*Figure 3.9*), a less than perfect repair of G:T mismatches implies a high mutation rate at CG dinucleotides, the majority of which are methylated. In fact, CG dinucleotides are subject to many more base substitutions than any other dinucleotide in the human genome, and most of these point mutations are C to T or G to A (the latter resulting from deamination of 5mC on the noncoding strand) [2]. As a consequence, CG dinucleotides are severely depleted and are found at only 20% of their expected frequency. It is worth mentioning that the hypermutability of CG has had important consequences for the design of mutation search strategies in eukaryotes. In order to be most efficient, CG-containing sites are often screened first, either by direct sequencing or by the use of restriction endonucleases with CG in their recognition sites (e.g. *Taq*I with recognition sequence TCGA).

By extrapolation, the rate of 5mC deamination *in vitro* in single-stranded DNA was estimated to be 10^{-9} per second under physiological conditions. Estimation of an *in vivo* rate has been hampered by the lack of sufficient sequence data of known evolutionary history. However, by consideration of the relative frequency at which CG mutations cause human inherited disease, an estimate of 5×10^{-16} per second was obtained (which is approximately 20 times the base mutation rate) [2].

In evolutionary comparisons, this figure is compatible with the CG distribution found in the globin genes and pseudogenes of several primate species. Furthermore, mathematical modeling has given an estimate of the time span required for the CG frequency to fall to its present low value.

52 mutation events were identified among 310 offspring, and only one of these was found to be of maternal origin. Segregation analysis of flanking markers did not reveal any concommitant crossing-over events. Further inference excluding unequal crossing-overs was found for three intronic $(CA)_n$ and $(TA)_n$ microsatellites within the cystic fibrosis (CFTR) gene on human chromosome 7, and for a short tetranucleotide repeat at locus DXS981 on the proximal long arm of the human X chromosome. However, in these studies *de novo* mutations could not be studied directly; instead, inference was indirect and came from the analysis of associated haplotypes.

In cases where the origin of the new allele was traceable, new mutant alleles at DXS981 varied by exactly one repeat unit. This result, together with those summarized above, suggests that the majority of length mutations at VNTR loci follow a so-called single-step mutation (SSM) model. This theoretical model implies that only small changes in repeat number occur at a time. The conclusions drawn from empirical data could be confirmed by computer simulations and theoretical considerations based on the SSM model. Valdes *et al.* [11] have demonstrated that the allele frequency distributions observed at 108 microsatellite loci were consistent with expectations, assuming that mutations cause an increase or decrease in the repeat number by one element. Furthermore, since no correlation was observed between the mean and variance in allele size, nor between the number of alleles and the mean allele size, the mutation rate at microsatellites must be independent of allele size.

Shriver and colleagues [12] have extended this type of analysis to loci with larger repeat units. Considering the number of alleles, the number of modes, the range in allele size and the heterozygosity reported for repetitive loci in the literature, these authors demonstrated that real data for microsatellites (1–5 bp repeat units) are closer to the simulation results of the SSM model than are minisatellites (15–70 bp repeat units). The parameter distributions of minisatellites exhibited similarity to the so-called infinite allele model, which in turn would be more appropriate for the explanation of mutations arising from unequal crossing-overs.

It should be noted in this context that consensus minisatellite DNA sequences (16 bp per repeat), introduced into human cells *in vitro* using a viral shuttle vector, increase the rate of recombination in the transfected cells by a factor of 13.5 [13]. This stimulation occurs at a distance and in both directions; expression was shown to be co-dominant. These findings also suggest a role of recombination for the mutagenesis of large repeat VNTRs.

3.4 Mitotic mutation of repetitive DNA

In the context of genetic individualization and kinship testing, meiotic (and thus heritable) mutations are of major interest, but in some medical contexts, somatic stability and mutability of repetitive DNA may also be important. This is especially the case for the diagnosis and characterization of tumor tissues (Section 2.3.2).

As already mentioned in Section 2.3.2, studies with oligonucleotide DNA probes, including $(CAC)_5$, $(CA)_8$ and $(GATA)_4$, have consistently failed to demonstrate any differences between DNA fingerprints from differentiated somatic tissues of one and the same individual [14]. However, in tumor tissues many changes in banding patterns have been observed, and tumor-specific bands have been found which may serve as markers both in the study of the pathogenetic mechanisms underlying the particular type of cancer, and in diagnostic procedures.

Similarly, Armour *et al.* [15] have shown that mutant minisatellite alleles are usually present at only a very low frequency in lymphoblastoid cell lines, but at much higher frequencies in tumor cells (most notably in gastrointestinal adenocarcinomas). Since mutant alleles in tumors were found at a dosage greater than that of the wild-type allele, this was held to indicate that virtually all mutant tumor alleles were the clonal result of a single mutational event. The incidence of somatic mutations in tumors varied from locus to locus, and the locus with the highest liability to germline mutation also exhibited the most pronounced somatic instability.

Jones and Nakamura [16] observed and characterized somatic mutations at three distinct loci containing $(CA)_n$ VNTRs. At one of these loci, studied in a three-generation pedigree, a new band generated from the same paternal allele was observed in four of six offspring. Since recurrent meiotic mutation was rather unlikely, this finding was consistent with an early mitotic mutation resulting in a substantial level of germline mosaicism in the father. A considerable number of somatic mutations at the two other loci were identified in a comparison of 25 cancers with their corresponding normal tissues.

A pronounced association between $(CA)_n$ repeat instability and tumor development was observed for hereditary nonpolyposis colorectal cancer (HNPCC), a syndrome that is characterized by a familial predisposition to colorectal carcinoma and extracolonic cancers of the gastrointestinal, urinary and female reproductive tracts. A gene responsible for HNPCC had been mapped previously to the short arm of human chromosome 2 by linkage analysis, and microsatellite instability has been thought to be due to a defect within that gene. Recently, Fishel *et al.* [17] identified a gene (MSH2) in the region 2p22–21 which exhibits sequence homology to a DNA mismatch repair gene of the yeast *Saccharomyces cerevisiae*. Since somatic as well as germline mutations of MSH2 were found to be associated with tumor development, this gene is likely to be implicated in the etiology of HNPCC. It has been postulated that MSH2 is capable of conferring a so-called mutator phenotype, either through an inherited lesion or by mutations acquired early in carcinogenesis.

Somatic mutation of repetitive DNA sequences is not limited to tumors but also occurs, albeit very rarely, in other tissues. Reports of early mitotic mutation events in humans are rare, although a very low level of mosaicism is routinely detected in human blood and sperm DNA. In mice, however, Kelly *et al.* [18] have identified a highly unstable minisatellite locus, *Ms6-hm*, by cross-hybridization with the human probe 33.6. A significant proportion of length mutations at *Ms6-hm* happen very early in mouse development, even before the somatic lineages are allocated, and the resulting animals are mosaics, with an almost equal number of cells carrying original and mutant alleles. It still remains to be seen, however, whether this phenomenon is unique to mice or can also occur in other species, including humans.

References

1. Kimura, M. (1991) *Proc. Natl Acad. Sci. USA*, **88**, 5969.
2. Cooper, D.N. and Krawczak, M. (1993) *Human Gene Mutation*. BIOS Scientific Publishers, Oxford.
3. Strachan, T. (1992) *The Human Genome*. BIOS Scientific Publishers, Oxford.
4. Pardue, M.L. (1991) *Cell*, **66**, 427.
5. Kunkel, T.A. and Alexander P.S. (1986) *J. Biol. Chem.*, **261**, 160.
6. Brown, T.C. and Jiricny, J. (1988) *Cell*, **54**, 705.
7. Loeb, L.A. (1985) *Cell* **40**, 483.
8. Jeffreys, A.J., Royle, N.J., Wilson, V. and Wong, Z. (1988) *Nature,* **332**, 278.
9. Jeffreys, A.J., Neumann, R. and Wilson,V. (1990) *Cell*, **60**, 473.
10. Vergnaud, G., Mariat, D., Apiou, F., Aurias, A., Lathrop, M. and Lauthier, V. (1991) *Genomics*, **11**, 135.
11. Valdes, A.M., Slatkin, M. and Freimer, N.B. (1993) *Genetics*, **133**, 737.
12. Shriver, M.D, Jin, L., Chakraborty, R. and Boerwinkle, E. (1993) *Genetics,* **134**, 983.
13. Wahls, W.P., Wallace, L.J. and Moore, P.D. (1990) *Cell*, **60**, 95.
14. Nürnberg, P., Roewer, L., Neitzel, H., Sperling, K., Pöpperl, A., Hundrieser, J., Pöche, H., Epplen, C., Zischler, H. and Epplen, J.T. (1989) *Hum. Genet.*, **84**, 75.
15. Armour, J.A., Patel, I., Thein, S.L., Fey, M.F. and Jeffreys, A.J. (1989) *Genomics*, **4**, 328.
16. Jones, M.H. and Nakamura, Y. (1992) *Hum. Mutat.*, **1**, 224.
17. Fishel, R., Lescoe, M.K., Rao, M.R.S., Copeland, N.G., Jenkins, N.A., Garber, J., Kane, M. and Kolodner, R. (1993) *Cell,* **75**, 1027.
18. Kelly, R., Bulfield, G., Collick, A., Gibbs, M. and Jeffreys, A. (1989) *Genomics*, **5**, 844.

Further reading

Boyer, S.H. (1987) *Birth Defects,* **23**, 191.

Holland, S.K. and Blake, C.C.F. (1987) *Biosystems,* **20**, 181.

Nei, M. (1975) *Molecular Population Genetics and Evolution*. Elsevier, Amsterdam.

Chapter 4

DNA typing to identify suspects

4.1 Population genetic aspects of DNA profiling

All forensic applications of DNA typing are based on the same principle. Since a considerable proportion of the genetic information embodied in a cell is host-specific and differs between any two individuals (with the exception only of monozygotic twins), analysis of this particular fraction of the genome allows unambiguous identification of any remaining biological trace. As long as DNA can be extracted and analyzed, the chance of success depends merely on the number and information content of the DNA systems tested. In forensic testing, small samples of somatic tissue (e.g. hair roots, sperm, fingernails) are analyzed, whereas in kinship testing (see Section 5.1) the haploid genome conveyed by a single gamete represents the issue of concern. In any case, the question to answer is whether or not a given individual under suspicion can be matched to material found at the site of the crime. Although positive identification alone is never a sufficient proof of guilt, DNA typing results nevertheless add substantially to the body of evidence that a court requires for sound decision making.

Although negative answers to the question of identity are usually quite easy to give, positive identification is much more difficult. When two DNA sequences exhibit more differences than are explicable by mutation alone, the suspect is definitely not the source of the material. The only problem here may be to obtain accurate estimates of the mutation rates involved. In cases of a match, however, when the degree of resemblance between trace and suspect DNA is compatible with identical origins, the question remains whether the observed coincidence could also be due to chance. Thus, estimates of genotype frequencies are required, and statistical analyses are involved.

4.1.1 The Hardy–Weinberg law

In 1908, the English mathematician Godfrey Hardy and the German physician Wilhelm Weinberg independently discovered and published a theoretical treatment that predicted, under the criteria listed below, the population frequencies of genotypes at a given locus. The formulae emerging from this approach have become recognized as the Hardy–Weinberg law.

First, the population of interest must be large enough to ensure that the allele frequencies among the germ cells constituting the seeds of the next generation approximate to the overall allele frequencies in the present generation. In Section 3.1.4 it was noted that in small populations this postulate may be violated due to gametic sampling variance. Secondly, there should be random mating, at least as far as genotypes of mating partners are concerned. Thirdly, mutation and selection are excluded, although in a more complex version of the Hardy–Weinberg law these parameters may also be considered. Finally, reproduction is assumed to take place in nonoverlapping generations; however, this restriction too can be dropped when more sophisticated formulae are being used.

Let us now assume that the genotypes at an autosomal, diallelic locus have population frequencies $u(A_1A_1)$, $2v(A_1A_2)$ and $w(A_2A_2)$, satisfying the equation $u + 2v + w = 1$. Then the allele frequencies in this population are $p_1 = u + v$ (i.e. the frequency of homozygotes for allele A_1 plus half the frequency of heterozygotes) and $p_2 = v + w$. Under the assumptions made above, six different mating types are possible with respect to the genotypes of mating partners. These are listed in *Table 4.1* together with their probabilities of occurrence. Also included in *Table 4.1* are the relative likelihoods of different offspring genotypes, depending on parental genotypes. The sum of these likelihoods, each of them weighted by the probability of the respective mating type, yields the overall genotype frequency among the progeny. For example, the offspring frequency of A_1A_1 is

$$u \cdot u + \tfrac{1}{2} \cdot 2 \cdot u \cdot 2v + \tfrac{1}{4} \cdot 2v \cdot 2v = u^2 + 2 \cdot u \cdot v + v^2 = (u + v)^2 = p_1^2,$$

which equals the square of the initial frequency of allele A_1. Similarly, the offspring frequency of A_2A_2 is p_2^2 and that of A_1A_2 is $2 \cdot p_1 \cdot p_2$, and it is easily seen that the allele frequencies in the new generation are the same as before. This implies that, whatever the genotype frequencies in the starting generation, one round of reproduction according to Hardy–Weinberg

Table 4.1: The Hardy–Weinberg law

Mating type	Probability	Offspring genotype		
		A_1A_1	A_1A_2	A_2A_2
$A_1A_1 \times A_1A_1$	$u \cdot u$	1	0	0
$A_1A_1 \times A_1A_2$	$2 \cdot u \cdot 2v$	½	½	0
$A_1A_1 \times A_2A_2$	$2 \cdot u \cdot w$	0	1	0
$A_1A_2 \times A_1A_2$	$2v \cdot 2v$	¼	½	¼
$A_1A_2 \times A_2A_2$	$2 \cdot w \cdot 2v$	0	½	½
$A_2A_2 \times A_2A_2$	$w \cdot w$	0	0	1

assumptions yields characteristic genotype frequencies which, from then on, remain unchanged. A population characterized by such genotype frequencies is said to be in Hardy–Weinberg equilibrium.

One potential application of the Hardy–Weinberg law is the estimation of allele frequencies for loci underlying phenotypes that are not co-dominant. For example, if an autosomal recessive disease has prevalence f, then f equals the frequency of homozygous carriers of the mutant allele, say, A_2. Therefore, $f = p_2^2$ under Hardy–Weinberg conditions and the frequency of A_2 can be estimated by the square root of f.

The Hardy–Weinberg law is easily extended to loci with more than two alleles: if alleles A_i and A_j have frequencies p_i and p_j respectively, the genotype frequency for A_iA_j is $2 \cdot p_i \cdot p_j$ and p_i^2 for A_iA_i. If sufficient data are available, the frequencies of genotypes can, of course, be estimated simply by counting them. However, it should be noted that the number of genotypes possible for n alleles equals $\frac{1}{2} \cdot n \cdot (n+1)$, which approximates to half the square of the allele number. Therefore, in the case of highly polymorphic loci, accurate frequency estimates can be obtained much more easily for alleles than for genotypes. If the population of interest fulfills (or approximates) Hardy–Weinberg conditions, the desired genotype frequency estimates can be computed from allele frequency estimates using formulae arising from *Table 4.1*.

4.1.2 Linkage disequilibrium

Compound genotypes convey much more genetic information than do single-locus data, and would therefore allow a much more refined identification of individuals. However, whereas genotype frequencies may be easy to evaluate for a single locus, the same exercise becomes almost unmanageable for genotypes comprising large numbers of loci. When the number of alleles per locus is (approximately) constant, then the number of possible genotypes increases exponentially with the number of loci included. In order to allow determination of frequency, genotypes at different loci must be stochastically independent of each other. This would imply that the frequency of a compound genotype amounts to the product of the frequencies of its constituents. In reality, however, a variety of factors ensure that this product rule is little more than a useful approximation to the truth. Genotypes at distinct loci are often far from being independent. Instead, some alleles show up together in the same cells more often (or less often) than expected by chance alone, meaning that there is *allelic association* between loci.

One possible reason for allelic association is linkage disequilibrium. As has been described in Section 1.2.4, the genetic material is not simply a pile of informational components that mix up freely and meet again in germ cells. The DNA is organized in chromosomes, long stretches of DNA that are wrapped in proteins and passed on to future generations almost intact. Therefore, alleles that have been resident on the same chromosome once should be so forever. Although meiotic recombination allows exceptions to this rule (Section 1.2.6), closely linked loci by definition only rarely undergo recombination, and their alleles have a high chance of remaining strung together in the same haplotype during meiosis. Thus, any initial over-representation of one allele in *cis* phase (i.e. on the same chromosome) with a particular allele of a second locus may be preserved for a considerable time. As a result, whenever one of the two alleles is present in a cell, genotypes including the other allele are seen more frequently than expected.

A variety of numerical quantities have been proposed in order to measure linkage disequilibrium between two loci with, say, alleles A_1, A_2 and B_1, B_2. One such measure is the so-called Yule coefficient, Φ, which is defined as the absolute value of the ratio:

$$(p_{1,1} - p_{1,2})/(p_{1,1} + p_{1,2} - 2 \cdot p_{1,1} \cdot p_{1,2}).$$

Here, $p_{1,1}$ and $p_{1,2}$ denote the frequency of allele A_1 on chromosomes bearing allele B_1 and B_2, respectively. Whereas $\Phi = 0$ is equivalent to the absence of linkage disequilibrium, $\Phi = 1$ is indicative of the maximum linkage disequilibrium possible assuming the actual allele frequencies. (It should be noted that the definition of Φ is independent of the choice of A_1 as a reference allele.) It is intuitively clear that Φ, in principle, increases with the closeness of linkage, but mechanisms like mutation, recombination and genetic drift may nevertheless distort or obscure this relationship.

In humans, one of the best characterized chromosomal regions with respect to linkage disequilibrium is that surrounding the gene responsible for Huntington disease (HD). Yule coefficients estimated for the HD gene and a number of surrounding marker loci [1] from the tip of the short arm of chromosome 4 are depicted in *Figure 4.1*. Although there is an obvious tendency to higher Yule coefficients in the vicinity of the HD gene, a large variation of Φ is also evident. At loci D4S180 and D4S95 (defined by probes L19ps11 and BS674, respectively), which map within a distance of less than 250 kb from the HD gene, restriction enzymes *Xmn*I and *Taq*I generate RFLPs that exhibit almost perfect equilibrium with HD (bottom squares in *Figure 4.1*). In contrast, the more distant BS731/*Sac*I-RFLP at locus D4S98 yields $\Phi = 0.46$.

4.1.3 Population stratification

Another phenomenon that is capable of causing allelic association and thus of violating the product rule is population stratification. A population initially thought to represent a homogenous collection of inter-marrying individuals may well turn out to be a mixture of separated sub-populations. When allele frequencies are considerably different from each other among these subpopulations, then the frequency of a particular allele at one locus depends on the corresponding subpopulation and, therefore, on the alleles present at other loci.

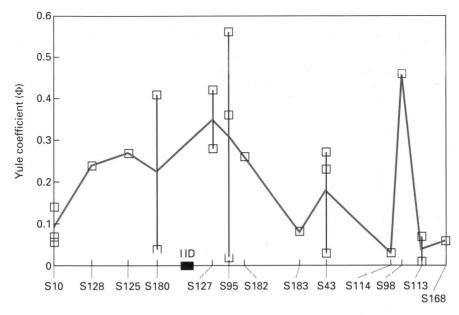

Figure 4.1: Patterns of linkage disequilibrium around the HD gene on human chromosome 4. A region spanning 2500 kb is displayed (marker loci are specified by their corresponding S numbers). At loci with Yule coefficients computed for more than one RFLP, represented by squares, the red line connects the mean coefficients.

In order to demonstrate the potential of population stratification for the generation of allelic association, let us consider again two loci with alleles A_1, A_2, and B_1, B_2. An example of haplotype frequencies observed in two distinct populations, P_1 and P_2, is summarized in *Table 4.2*.

When each population is considered separately, Yule coefficients are zero, indicating the absence of linkage disequilibrium. However, when the two groups make up equal proportions of a larger population, and when this large population is misinterpreted as being homogenous, then allelic

Table 4.2: Allelic association due to population substructuring

Population	Haplotype	Frequency	Yule coefficient
P_1	A_1B_1	1/25	0.00
	A_1B_2	4/25	
	A_2B_1	4/25	
	A_2B_2	16/25	
P_2	A_1B_1	16/25	0.00
	A_1B_2	4/25	
	A_2B_1	4/25	
	A_2B_2	1/25	
$\frac{1}{2} \cdot P_1 + \frac{1}{2} \cdot P_2$	A_1B_1	17/50	0.25
	A_1B_2	8/50	
	A_2B_1	8/50	
	A_2B_2	17/50	

association arises. Although all alleles are equally frequent in the mixed population, allele A_1 occurs more often on the same chromosome together with allele B_1 than with allele B_2. Therefore, genotypes including A_1 are likely to be accompanied by genotypes including B_2.

Population stratification can also result in a deviation from Hardy–Weinberg equilibrium. This is illustrated in *Table 4.3*, listing the genotype frequencies to be expected in the above example when both subpopulations fulfill Hardy–Weinberg conditions at locus A. Although each subpopulation alone is in equilibrium, the combined population exhibits considerable heterozygote deficiency.

Table 4.3: Hardy–Weinberg disequilibrium in a mixed population

Genotype	Frequency in $\frac{1}{2} \cdot P_1 + \frac{1}{2} \cdot P_2$ population	
	Observed	Expected
A_1A_1	34/100	25/100
A_1A_2	32/100	50/100
A_2A_2	34/100	25/100

4.2 Quantifying the evidence

If decisions must be made in the face of uncertainty, common sense tells us that we should acquire in advance as much information as possible about the object in question. When a court has to decide whether a given individual is deemed a murderer, a rapist, or the father of a disowned child, genetic experts may contribute such information.

Biological traces often contain DNA or proteins still amenable to molecular analysis, and genotypes usually present themselves in non-random relationship between parents and their offspring. The question to answer is whether any match or relationship is a proof of guilt, or whether it could also be due to chance alone. Any test system should aim to provide the court with convincing evidence in favor of one of these two alternatives, but an unequivocal answer can be given only rarely. Evidence is thus phrased in terms of probabilities, allowing the remaining uncertainty to be at least quantified.

4.2.1 Bayes' rule

The quantity that is of interest to those involved in a criminal case or paternity dispute is $P(H|E)$, the conditional probability of an hypothesis (H), reflecting, for example, the accusation of guilt, identity or paternity, given the expert's evidence (E). This figure is usually unknown and needs to be calculated from other numerical values applying Bayes' rule, as follows:

$$P(H|E) = \frac{P(H) \cdot P(E|H)}{P(H) \cdot P(E|H) + P(nH) \cdot P(E|nH)} = \frac{1}{1 + P(nH)/P(H) \cdot P(E|nH)/P(E|H)}.$$

The central parameter in which the expert's evidence is condensed is the so-called likelihood ratio (L), which equals $P(E|nH)/P(E|H)$. Here, $P(E|H)$ and $P(E|nH)$ denote the likelihoods (or conditional probabilities) of the evidence under the assumption of the hypothesis being true or false, respectively (thus, nH stands for 'not H'). The likelihood ratio is thus a measure of how much more likely the evidence would be if the defendant were, in fact, innocent. A small value of L consequently argues in favor of guilt, whereas a large L value provides evidence against the hypothesis that the suspect is guilty. Thus, a major goal for rational decision-making usually lies in finding a meaningful threshold, L_o, such that the suspect is acquitted whenever L is larger than L_o, and found guilty if L is smaller than L_o [2].

$P(H)$ and $P(nH)$ denote the prior probabilities of the hypothesis being true or false, respectively. These probabilities allow for evidence which, in addition to that provided by the expert, might also be considered in decision-making. If, for example, a defendant is able to convince the court that he had been out of town at the time of the murder, then even a very small likelihood ratio can be outweighed by this fact. Prior probabilities may either be purely intuitive or may stem from empirical studies. Although empirical figures appear to be scientifically more substantiated, their reliability and their relevance to an individual case may be questioned as much as for intuitive estimates.

Use of Bayes' rule will now be illustrated for an identification method that has been in common use long before DNA testing became feasible: the ABO blood group system. Let us assume that both a crime sample and a suspect have blood group type B (this is the evidence, E), and the hypothesis of the prosecuting attorney is that the crime sample indeed comes from that suspect. Calculation of $P(E|H)$ is comparatively easy. Provided no laboratory error has occurred, suspect and sample must necessarily match in the case of guilt; that is, $P(E|H) = 1$.

The likelihood under the assumption of innocence, however, is more problematic. The true likelihood $P(E|nH)$ should equal the average $P(E|H)$ among all potential perpetrators and, since $P(E|H)$ is either zero or unity, amounts to the frequency of blood group B within this particular subpopulation. The problem now arises as to which population to choose. This controversial issue is discussed in more detail in Section 4.2.5, but for the sake of simplicity, let us consider all Central Europeans as potential culprits. In Central Europe, the frequency of blood group B is approximately 5% [3] and, thus, $P(E|nH) = 0.05$.

Probabilities of guilt, $P(H|E)$, resulting from different ratios of prior probabilities, $P(nH)/P(H)$, are summarized in *Table 4.4*. As shown, even when prior odds of guilt are 50:50, which may be thought of as adopting a 'neutral' position, the posterior probability is still as large as 95.24%. However, it must be emphasized again that this result depends critically upon the choice of the underlying population. Had the crime taken place, for example, in Northern India, where the frequency of blood group B is approximately 40% [3], then the posterior probability of guilt would have been three times smaller in the case of 90:10 prior odds. This finding is also intuitively apparent because a higher population frequency for the sample blood type must always increase the chance of a random match between sample and suspect.

Table 4.4: Probabilities of guilt, $P(H|E)$, at various ratios of prior probabilities

Prior probability $P(nH):P(H)$	Posterior probability, $P(H|E)$	
	Central Europe	Northern India
1:99	0.9994	0.9960
10:90	0.9945	0.9574
50:50	0.9524	0.7143
90:10	0.6897	0.2174
99:1	0.1681	0.0246

For details, see text.

4.2.2 Likelihoods for single-locus DNA profiles

Various techniques are available for DNA typing at single loci. The majority of polymorphisms are detected by virtue of sequence alterations at or around restriction enzyme recognition sites (RFLPs; see Section 2.2.1). Such changes either affect the presence or absence of a particular restriction site or introduce an insertion or a deletion between them. In any case, DNA fragments of variable lengths become apparent using suitable detection systems. RFLPs are not rare, being distributed throughout the genome approximately every 200–300 bp [4], and they may be detected using either genes or arbitrary DNA segments as hybridization probes. However, RFLPs do not appear to occur randomly and some restriction enzymes, most notably *Msp*I and *Taq*I which contain the hypermutable CG dinucleotide in their recognition sequences (see Section 3.2.4), detect more polymorphic variation than enzymes which do not recognize CG-containing sequences. At present, well over 7000 RFLPs have been documented in databases such as the Genome Database in Baltimore (maintained at Johns Hopkins University).

Increasingly, DNA profiling as well as gene mapping is using the new class of highly polymorphic mini- and microsatellites which give rise to VNTR polymorphisms. As outlined in detail in Section 2.2.1, these multiallelic polymorphisms are characterized by variable numbers of short clustered repeat units (the core motifs), and many of them can be analyzed by PCR. With this technique, DNA fragments are generated by enzymatic amplification of a region spanning the polymorphism (see Chapter 2.1.7). Thus, digestion with restriction enzymes is no longer required and in many instances even hybridization has become superfluous. DNA fragments are generated in such high copy numbers that they are visible directly on an electrophoretic gel (*Figure 4.2*). Due to variation in repeat

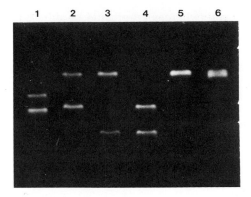

Figure 4.2: Direct analysis by PCR, followed by agarose gel electrophoresis, of a hexanucleotide VNTR (D11S533) on human chromosome 11. Each of the six lanes contains amplified DNA from a different individual.

copy number, amplification products of different length are obtained which thereby define an amplification fragment length polymorphism (AmpFLP). Since the repeat flanking region is usually shorter, AmpFLPs allow a better discrimination between alleles than VNTR-RFLPs, especially when the latter comprise large fragments and/or when their length differences are small.

Most conventional RFLPs (other than VNTRs) comprise poly-morphic DNA fragments (alleles) so different in length that they can be distinguished from one another without ambiguity, but the situation may be more problematic with many VNTR-RFLPs. As long as the genotype of a given individual can be determined, the probabilities of any match to a criminal trace are calculated as explained for the ABO blood group system in Section 4.2.1. Whilst $P(E|H)$ equals unity again (mutations rendering this assertion somewhat imprecise have been considered in Section 3.4), $P(E|nH)$ equals the frequency of the corresponding RFLP genotype (the evidence E) in the appropriate population.

However, since some VNTR core motifs are as short as two or three base pairs (e.g. CA or CAC), alleles which differ only by a small number of repeats, say one or two, are often impossible to distinguish by standard gel electrophoretic means. Although this problem may be avoided by the use of probes for larger core sequences, it nevertheless applies to a considerable proportion of routinely employed VNTRs. Furthermore, fragment length measurement is affected by experimental variation that can easily mimic or obscure minor allelic differences. In other words, when direct sequencing or lane-by-lane comparison with appropriate standards is not feasible, measurement errors of VNTR alleles can be larger than length differences.

In such instances, alleles of mini- and microsatellites must be viewed as representing continuous rather than discrete entities, which implies that individual alleles and genotypes cannot be defined. Electrophoretic bands which correspond to one and the same DNA fragment may occupy different positions in different gel lanes, whereas fragments of different length can co-migrate. Thus, it is necessary to establish reasonable criteria for the declaration of a match between electrophoretic bands.

One commonly adopted match criterion is based on the average fragment length measure [5]. If the length measures corresponding to two bands under consideration are denoted by x and y, then a match is declared whenever

$$2 \cdot |x - y|/(x + y) < C,$$

where C is a threshold determined on the basis of either empirical data or theoretical considerations or both. In extensive duplicate DNA analyses, Evett and Gill [5] found $C = 0.024$ to be a reasonable value, whereas others have suggested more stringent boundaries (see below).

In terms of population genetics, use of quasi-continous allele distributions means that neither the Hardy–Weinberg equilibrium nor allelic association can be precisely tested for in a strictly statistical sense. However, methods have been suggested to account for continuous allele spectra in likelihood calculations.

4.2.3 The binning approach

For highly polymorphic VNTRs with sometimes up to several hundred alleles, the distribution of fragment length is quasi-continuous rather than discrete and, instead of allele frequencies, only frequencies of size ranges can be determined. Identification of a particular allele is replaced by naming the size range, or 'bin', that includes it. Since length measurement is subject to experimental errors, bins must not be too small; otherwise there may be a considerable chance of a fragment being assigned to the wrong bin. On the other hand, the larger the bin, the higher its population frequency will be. This means that large bins reduce the power of identification provided by a match.

It should be noted in this context that the principle underlying binning (i.e. pooling of alleles) is not at all novel [6]. For example, alleles A at the ABO locus, are heterogenous (subtypes A_1 and A_2 exist), and in the in-direct diagnosis of many monogenic disorders (e.g. cystic fibrosis, hemophilia B) what has been correctly dealt with for many years as the 'disease allele' turned out to comprise hundreds of different sequence alterations.

For theoretical reasons, it can be assumed that fragment length measurement errors follow a Gaussian distribution with a mean of 0. This implies that only 0.25% of errors will exceed three times its standard deviation (sd), and therefore ±3 sd of the measurement error has been adopted as a reasonable minimum bin size [7]. Experiments have revealed that the sd usually equals 0.5–1.0% of the measured fragment size [7,8].

Bins can be defined with either fixed or floating boundaries. With the 'fixed bin' approach (which the FBI use [8]), the reasonable size range for a bin is determined in advance by the analysis of molecular standards (e.g.

restriction enzyme digests of sequenced viral DNA), and these boundaries, once established, are adopted for each VNTR of interest. In order to cover a suitable number of alleles, fixed bins which are larger than ±3 SD of the length measurement error are usually chosen. In the FBI database, bin sizes range from 6% to 12% of the intra-bin fragment size. *Figure 4.3* illustrates fixed binning by US Black population data for locus D14S13 [8]. For example, if an individual is heterozygous for two fragments measuring 4.1 kb and 8.0 kb, these fragments would fall into the shaded bins of *Figure 4.3*, and the genotype probability would be calculated as twice the product of the bin frequencies, i.e. $2 \cdot 0.43 \cdot 0.10 = 0.086$. In the same diagram, upper 95% confidence limits of the bin frequencies are also shown, and it has been suggested by some research workers that these figures should be included instead of point estimates in the calculation of match probabilities. However, whilst this action may be meaningful for allele frequencies, it appears to be over conservative and unnecessary in the case of bins [5, 8].

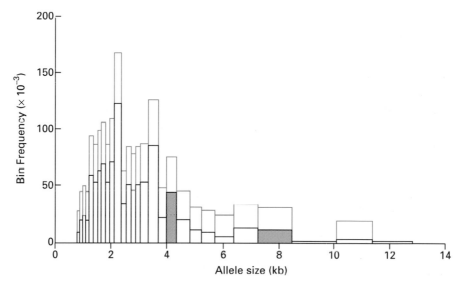

Figure 4.3: Fixed bin frequencies for locus D14S13 in a US Black population. The vertical lines demarcate each bin, and the upper 95% confidence limits of bin frequencies are shown in orange. The shaded bars are described in the text. Data derived from Ref. [8].

In order to avoid underestimation of bin frequencies due to sampling variation, the FBI statisticians have suggested that bins observed less than five times in a particular population of sufficient size should be combined with a neighboring bin. Finally, whenever the allele size measured in an actual case is close to one of the boundaries, and when the adjacent bin is more frequent, the frequency of this neighboring bin should be included in the likelihood calculation. This procedure further reduces the risk of over-estimating the posterior probability of guilt.

'Floating bins' are defined by boundaries that are located at fixed distances from the actual measured allele size (e.g. ±3 sD). Since the boundaries of a bin are thus not known in advance, its frequency needs to be determined for each individual case. The use of floating bins for locus D17S79 is depicted in *Figure 4.4*. The frequency data included here are from a sample of 295 Hispanics used by Lifecodes Inc., Valhalla, New York, testifying in one of the most famous cases ever solved by DNA typing, 'New York versus Castro'. A suspect named Castro was accused of murdering a Bronx woman and her daughter. Blood stains on Castro's watch were analyzed and fragments from at least two loci, D17S79 and D2S44, were declared to match the woman's blood rather than his own [7]. At D17S79, the victim's DNA fragments measured 3.464 kb and 3.869 kb, whereas the blood stain typed 3.541 kb and 3.877 kb. Bins were defined covering ±3·0.6% = ±1.8% of the victim's allele sizes (*Figure 4.4*), and the corresponding bin frequencies were determined to be 15.5% and 11.1%, respectively. Therefore, the probability of a random match was 2·0.155·0.111 = 0.0344 assuming that, under Hardy-Weinberg conditions, bin phenotypes are paired as randomly as alleles. At D2S44, both the victim and the blood stain were found to be 'homozygous' for a bin of frequency 0.049, resulting in a random match probability of $0.049^2 = 0.0024$. Thus, the combined likelihood ratio was 0.0344·0·0024, that is, approximately 1:12 000 in favor of identity.

However, it should be noted that, at D17S79, the 3.541 kb fragment from the blood stain is larger than 3.464 + 0.018·3.464 = 3.526 kb, and

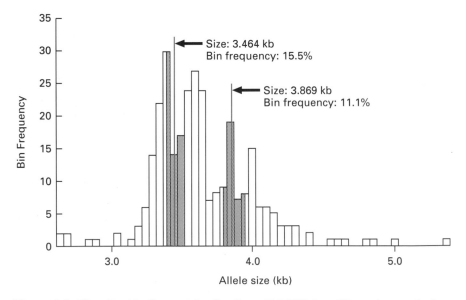

Figure 4.4: Floating bin frequencies for locus D17S79 in a Hispanic population. Bins are depicted as orange areas and have been defined for two alleles of a murder victim reported in the case 'New York versus Castro'. Data derived from Ref. [7].

therefore actually lies outside the floating bin. That a match between victim and stain has nevertheless been declared by Lifecodes Inc. has been criticized by Berry [7], who stated that "it is logically important to use the same criteria in deciding whether a suspect sample [...] matches a crime sample as in deciding what proportion of the general population matches."

Although the binning approach is held by many to be conservative, this is not generally true. As already mentioned above, measurement errors follow a Gaussian distribution so that values close to a true allele size are in fact more likely than distant observations, such as observations 3 SDs apart. When the empirically determined bell shape of the error distribution is allowed for in the Castro case, the numerical results change dramatically. Instead of 1:12000 in favor, a likelihood ratio of 60:1 against identity is obtained [7]. Because of the serious doubts and uncertainties that remained, the judge ruled the DNA analysis by Lifecodes Inc. an inadmissable proof of identity in the Castro case. Nevertheless, justice took its course and, eventually, the suspect pleaded guilty.

4.2.4 Is the multiplication rule valid?

In late 1991, the scientific community witnessed an intense debate on whether the common practice of quantifying DNA evidence (outlined in detail in the previous sections) is indeed valid. An article appeared in *Science* [9] in which two eminent American geneticists, Richard Lewontin and Daniel Hartl, seriously criticized the use of the multiplication rule for calculating match probabilities. They challenged the assumption that major racial groups are genetically homogenous (see Section 4.1.3 for the relevance of the homogeneity assumption in this context). Instead, it was claimed that 'Caucasian', 'Black' and 'Hispanic' are merely synonyms for amalgams of genetically diverse subpopulations. In an immigrant community like the US, genetic substructures were to be expected for a number of reasons. First, there has been substantial genetic differentiation among the immigrant populations. Caucasians, for example, comprise individuals from Britain, where the B allele of the ABO blood group system occurs at a frequency of 5–10%, as well as people from Russia, where B is as common as 30%. The Lu^a allele of the Lutheran blood group even varies within Britain, from less than 0.5% in Wales to 4.5% in Ireland. Lewontin and Hartl argued that similar or even more pronounced differences should apply to VNTRs because the lack of selection pressure renders these loci more sensitive to chance fluctuations in allele frequency. In their view, Hispanics constitute an even more spectacular 'biological hotchpotch', grouping Cubans of mainly African ancestry together with, for example, Guatemalan Indians. Secondly, most immigrants came to the US quite recently (mainly during the first half of the twentieth century), leaving very little time for the US population to become sufficiently panmictic. Finally, mating in reality is far from being 'at random'. Like ethnicity and religion, propinquity (the tendency to marry the girl next door) contributes significantly to the maintenance of population stratification [9].

The authors suggested that the dilemma be resolved by avoiding the multiplication rule. Instead, the frequency of the combined VNTR profile in the appropriate database should be determined, and used as an estimate of the match probability. In order to be conservative, a match probability of $1/x$ should be adopted for unobserved profiles, where x is the total number of individuals present in the database. Alternatively, the authors envisaged the current method being fixed by the incorporation of more detailed data. If allele frequencies were known for the relevant ethnic subgroups, the multiplication rule could be applied *within* these groups, avoiding the aforementioned problems to a considerable extent.

Despite these points, in the same issue of *Science*, both the arguments and the supporting data of Lewontin and Hartl were criticized by two other population geneticists, Ranajit Chakraborty and Kenneth Kidd [6]. These authors insisted on the necessity "to draw the distinction between exact values and valid estimates", and their claim was that every estimate which deliberately favors the defendant is acceptable. They said that, for VNTR data, possible errors are more likely to average out rather than to reinforce, and that the systematic overestimates of allele frequencies provided by the binning approach ensure that the resulting *combined* estimates are still larger than the best estimates of the true genotype frequencies.

That population affiliation is indeed of minor importance was documented by a reclassification experiment. The probabilities of the VNTR profiles of 2046 individuals in the FBI database were calculated once on the basis of Caucasian population data and once based on bin frequencies observed among US Blacks. The result is depicted in *Figure 4.5* in the format of a two-dimensional scatter diagram. Perfect agreement between the original and the faked genotype probabilities would be reflected by all points lying on the 45° line. As is evident, no noteworthy differences were detected between the two groups of estimates.

Contrary to the opinion expressed by Lewontin and Hartl, Chakraborty and Kidd also believe that there has been sufficient migration across ethnic and religious boundaries to homogenize populations. They refer to the literature on blood groups and protein markers which has not indicated, in their view, "any appreciable departures of single or multilocus [in the sense of combined single-locus] genotype frequencies from the ones predicted with the Hardy–Weinberg and multiplication rules". This assertion received further support from a study of the VNTR databases of both the FBI (covering five loci) and Lifecodes Inc. (three loci) [10]. Among the Hispanic profiles logged in the FBI database, three pairs of loci exhibited an association of match probabilities (D1S7-

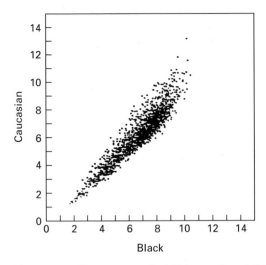

Figure 4.5: Genotype probabilities at four VNTR loci for 2046 Americans. Probabilities are displayed on a $-\log$ scale and were calculated once from US Black (horizontal axis) and once from Caucasian allele frequencies (vertical axis). Reproduced from Chakraborty and Kidd (1991) with permission from The American Association for the Advancement of Science.

D4S139, D4S139-D10S7, D4S139-D17S79), but allowing for multiple testing (10 comparisons) rendered these findings as insignificant as all other comparisons.

Finally, the approach suggested by Lewontin and Hartl to avoid the multiplication rule was rejected by Chakraborty and Kidd because, in most cases, it would fail to reflect the true significance of a match. For example, 20 bins per locus would give approximately 2×10^9 possible four-locus DNA profiles, but the minimum frequency estimate that could possibly be obtained from 500 individuals is as large as $1/500 = 2 \times 10^{-3}$.

4.2.5 Which population?

Another issue of concern among those involved in forensic DNA typing is how to choose, in the case of a match, an appropriate population for comparison and calculation of the match probability. If all potential culprits are available for analysis, then DNA testing is merely an exclusion exercise. Provided: (1) that the loci under consideration are numerous and sufficiently polymorphic, and (2) that kinship and inbreeding are negligible, mismatches will be so frequent for all but one suspect that the true perpetrator can be easily identified. In most cases, however, only a single suspect is tested, and without eye-witness or other reliable evidence, not even the race of the criminal is known. On the other hand, matching probabilities depend on the underlying allele and genotype frequencies (and therefore population), and if there is considerable ethnic variability, the choice of the database used to evaluate a match is an ethically significant action. One and the same sample DNA profile may be rare in one population, and therefore incriminate the suspect, but may be orders of magnitude more common in another.

Morton [11] has rightly pointed out that the ethnic origin of the suspect is usually irrelevant to the likelihood ratio, and that the choice of the reference population should not be the expert's major concern. Since match probabilities are calculated under the assumption of *innocence*, the only argument for using allele frequencies from the suspect's population would be courtesy. There are good reasons to assume that under ethnic heterogeneity the suspect's profile is more frequent in his own population than in many (if not most) of the others.

Since the conservative character attributed to data from the suspect's population is not always guaranteed, a so-called 'ceiling' approach has been suggested for the determination of suitable allele frequencies. The basic idea of this proposal, which was recorded in the National Research Council's (NRC) report on DNA fingerprinting in May 1992 [12], is as follows. In each of 15–20 populations (e.g. English, Russian, Indian, African), a total of 100 individuals should be typed for all loci of interest. Then, when scoring a combined genotype, the maximum allele frequency estimated among these groups should be employed for each individual locus. This would imply that "a forensic genotype probability could be a product of a Navajo allele probability, a few Russian allele probabilities, a West African allele probability, and so on" [12]. Further, a minimum probability of 5% was regarded as mandatory for each allele and should be substituted whenever a frequency estimate is smaller in all groups.

Although the ceiling principle appears sensible at first glance, it has nevertheless provoked a wave of criticism [11–13]. First, it ignores the fact that a DNA profile is always contributed by a single person and not by a mixture of individuals of different ethnic backgrounds. Therefore, it is more meaningful to use the maximum allele frequency product obtained from one of the databases as a combined genotype probability, instead of multiplying the locus-wise maxima. Secondly, the ceiling principle ignores the fact that frequency differences are likely to average out. US population geneticist Bruce Weir said that "it cannot be true that all alleles at one locus in one population are more frequent than all those in another population. Over loci, it is observed that some alleles are more frequent in the first of two populations, while others are less frequent" [13]. Finally, the arbitrary boundary of 5% is as difficult to justify as the NRC's recommended sample size of 100 individuals per population. In the case of a highly polymorphic locus with alleles that are rare all over the world, 5% may be inappropriately large, while a sample of 100 people may turn out to be too small.

Nevertheless, it should be remembered that the problem of ethnic variability is not at all specific to DNA testing. Rather it is central to any test system (e.g. blood groups, isoenzymes, HLA) that relies on otherwise infrequent matches between suspects and samples or traces. The great advance contributed by DNA technology lies in its high discriminative power and the low chances of fortuitous matches. Thus, instead of enforcing the need to control for ethnic origin, DNA typing is more likely to render the question 'Which population?' more and more irrelevant.

References

1. MacDonald, M.E., Lin, C., Srinidhi, L., Bates, G., Altherr, M., Whaley, W.L., Lehrach, H., Wasmuth, J. and Gusella, J.F. (1991) *Am. J. Hum. Genet.*, **49**, 723.
2. Krawczak, M. and Schmidtke, J. (1993) *J. Forens. Sci.*, **37**, 1525.
3. Vogel, F. and Motulsky, A. (1979) In *Human Genetics.* Springer, Berlin, p. 405.
4. Cooper, D.N., Smith, B.A., Cooke, H.J., Niemann, S. and Schmidtke, J. (1985) *Hum. Genet.*, **69**, 201.
5. Evett, I.W. and Gill, P. (1991) *Electrophoresis*, **12**, 226.
6. Chakraborty, R. and Kidd, K.K. (1991) *Science*, **254**, 1735.
7. Berry, D.A. (1992) in *DNA on Trial* (P.R. Billings, ed.). Cold Spring Harbor Laboratory Press, Cold Spring Harbor.
8. Budowle, B., Giusti, A.M., Waye, J.S., Baechtel, F.S., Fourney, R.M., Adams, D.E., Presley, L.A., Deadman, H.A. and Monson, K.L. (1991) *Am. J. Hum. Genet.*, **48**, 841.
9. Lewontin, R.C and Hartl, D.L (1991) *Science*, **254**, 1745.
10. Risch, N.J. and Devlin, B. (1992) *Science*, **255**, 717.
11. Morton, N.E. (1993) *Eur. J. Hum. Genet.*, **1**, 172.
12. Devlin, B., Risch, N.J and Roeder, K. (1993) *Science*, **259**, 748.
13. Weir, B.S. (1993) *Am. J. Hum. Genet.*, **52**, 437.

Chapter 5

DNA typing to establish relationships

5.1 Kinship testing

The previous chapter focused mainly on determining the origin of crime samples or traces but, for very obvious reasons, DNA typing has also found its way into kinship testing. Since DNA is heritable and highly specific to an individual (except for monozygotic twins), DNA profiles represent an excellent means of resolving genealogical problems.

In the forensic context, conditional probabilities of the observed molecular evidence given guilt (or identity), $P(E|H)$, and innocence (or non-identity), $P(E|nH)$, have been shown to be relevant (Section 4.2.1). Similar parameters can also be defined for kinship testing. However, in this case the evidence comprises not just two DNA profiles (suspect and sample, checked for a match) but can include test results for a large number of individuals. In paternity cases, for example, testing is usually performed at least on the child, mother and putative father, and the decision has to be made between paternity and non-paternity. In general, kinship testing can involve a virtually unlimited number of hypotheses, each characterized by a particular relationship or pedigree structure. This is exemplified in *Figure 5.1* for a paternity case (a) and a complex situation involving possible incest (b), both typed for a locus with alleles A_1 and A_2.

In the first case, hypothesis H comprises true paternity, while nH means that the putative father is unrelated to both mother and child. Since the mother is homozygous A_1A_1, the molecular evidence, E, constitutes the offspring's A_2 allele. According to Mendelian rules, the likelihood of a child, II.1, being heterozygous is 1/2 under the assumption of paternity. Assuming nonpaternity, the paternal germ cell must have carried allele A_2 and therefore the likelihood under nH equals the population frequency (p_2) of A_2. So the likelihood ratio $L = P(E|nH)/P(E|H) = 2p_2$, which is proportional to p_2. Thus, evidence in favor of paternity becomes more and more convincing as the frequency of allele A_2 decreases.

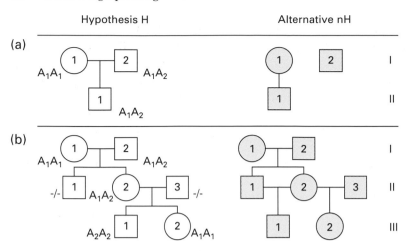

Figure 5.1: Paternity testing in (a) a trio comprising mother, child and alleged father, and (b) in a complex case involving possible incest. Females are symbolized by circles; squares represent male individuals.

The second case deals with the question whether a boy (III.1) is the son of his social father (II.3) or stems instead from an incestuous contact of his mother (II.2) and his uncle (II.1). Both putative fathers were unavailable for testing, so the sister (III.2) and the maternal grandparents (I.1 and I.2) were tested. From the typing results (*Figure 5.1*) it is evident that under the assumption of paternity (hypothesis H), the social father must have been heterozygous A_1A_2. The frequency of this genotype is $2p_1p_2$, assuming Hardy–Weinberg equilibrium. The genotype of the uncle is irrelevant in this case, so that he contributes a factor of unity to the probability. Since the probability of two discordant, homozygous offspring is $1/16$,

$$P(E|H) = 2p_1p_2 \cdot 1/16.$$

Under the alternative of incest (nH), the uncle must have been heterozygous, because he has inherited A_1 from his mother and has passed A_2 to his son III.1. Therefore, he must have inherited A_2 rather than A_1 from his father, which gives him a genotype probability of $1/2$. The probability of the homozygous genotype A_2A_2 of III.1 is then $1/4$, if both parents (II.1 and II.2) are assumed to be heterozygous. The social father can be homozygous, A_1A_1, or heterozygous, A_1A_2, resulting in a probability of the A_1A_1 genotype of his daughter, III.2, of either $1/2$ or $1/4$, respectively. Therefore,

$$P(E|nH) = 1/2 \cdot 1/4 \cdot [1/2 \cdot p_1^2 + 1/4 \cdot 2p_1p_2] = p_1/16,$$

because $p_1 + p_2 = 1$. The likelihood ratio $L = P(E|nH)/P(E|H) = 1/2p_2$, which is the inverse of the ratio determined in case (a). Thus, incest becomes more likely as the frequency of allele A_2 decreases.

For the hypothetical examples of *Figure 5.1*, likelihoods could still be determined analytically. However, in more complex pedigrees with critical individuals missing, or when linkage between loci needs to be considered, this is almost impossible. In such situations, computer programs are required which are able to handle phenotypic and genotypic information obtained in large families. Such programs exist and they almost invariably make use of a method for complex pedigree analysis that was described in detail by Elston and Stewart in 1971 [1].

Briefly, an individual's phenotype, ϕ, is assumed to be due to one out of a total of n possible genotypes g_i. If $P(\phi|g_i)$ denotes the penetrance (i.e. the probability of observing phenotype ϕ given genotype g_i) then the likelihood of observing a single individual with phenotype ϕ and genotype g_i is

$$P(g_i) \cdot P(\phi|g_i).$$

Here, $P(g_i)$ denotes the population frequency of genotype g_i. However, if the parental genotypes are known or if the consideration of ancestors is necessary in order to link individuals formally to remote relatives, the population frequency $P(g_i)$ is replaced by $P(g_i|g_m,g_f)$, which is the conditional probability of genotype g_i given parental genotypes g_m and g_f, respectively. In this case, the likelihood of observing a single individual with phenotype ϕ and genotype g_i is

$$P(g_i|g_m,g_f) \cdot P(\phi|g_i).$$

The phenotype likelihood of the whole family is obtained as follows. If genotypes are known for all family members, then the total likelihood equals the product of the individual likelihoods mentioned above. Individuals who lack phenotype information do not contribute to the likelihood and, consequently, $P(\phi|g_i)$ is replaced by unity for them. If genotypes are unknown for, say, k individuals, then these individuals are assigned each of the n possible genotypes once, and the overall likelihood equals the sum of the likelihood products resulting for each of the n^k different genotype constellations possible in that family.

5.2 Multilocus DNA fingerprinting

Previous sections focused on test systems employing single-locus probes or primers; that is, DNA fragments that hybridize only once per genome with sufficient specificity, and thus pin-point polymorphisms at a single locus only. Even when different RFLPs can be detected at a given locus using the same probe (but different enzymes), close linkage between these variants and the consequent high chance of exhibiting allelic association renders their combined informativity limited.

Multilocus probes, in contrast, hybridize to many different sites in the genome and are thus capable of identifying polymorphism at many DNA loci at a time (Section 2.2.3). When genomic DNA is enzymatically digested and size-separated by gel electrophoresis, hybridization with a multilocus probe yields a hybridization pattern resembling the barcode used to identify goods in supermarkets (*Figure 5.2*). It should be noted that the term 'DNA fingerprint' was originally intended exclusively for this type of hybridization pattern.

The high information content of a multilocus DNA fingerprint is immediately evident. Among the three suspects typed in *Figure 5.2*, individual 1 is easily identified as the source of the specimen, which illustrates that qualitative decision-making from multilocus DNA fingerprints does not usually pose any problems. However, whereas typing results for single-locus probes can be analyzed formally as co-dominant Mendelian traits (see Section 4.2.2), the quantitative analysis of multilocus DNA fingerprints is more difficult. This is true not only for technical

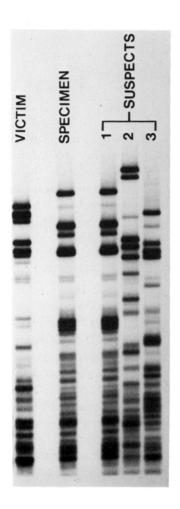

Figure 5.2: Multilocus DNA fingerprint of a victim, a specimen and three suspects. Photograph courtesy of Cellmark Diagnostics, Abingdon, Oxfordshire, UK.

reasons but also because of some peculiarities that are intrinsic to the method itself.

(1) Autoradiographic bands that are allelic (i.e. generated by two different fragments from the homologs of one and the same DNA locus) are unlikely to be recognized as such unless laborious experiments are performed. Furthermore, both alleles of a given locus may not actually be visible in the analyzed portion of a gel. As a consequence, definition of alleles or bins and the determination of their frequencies is impossible.

(2) Nonallelic fragments of similar size and molecular weight can produce bands that are close to each other or even coincide.

(3) Whether a band represents heterozygosity or homozygosity at the underlying DNA locus is difficult to determine.

(4) Genetic linkage between the loci detected by a multilocus probe reduces the actual information conveyed by a DNA fingerprint, and this problem is difficult to account for in a satisfying formal manner.

5.2.1 Quantitative approaches based on band-sharing

In the context of kinship testing, several approaches have been reported of computational analysis of multilocus DNA fingerprints. These are reviewed briefly in the following paragraphs. Many of these methods are numerically equivalent, or yield almost identical results and so only a few of them will be considered in more detail. The most important parameter of multilocus DNA fingerprints is the band-sharing rate, β_{ij}, of two individuals i and j. This figure equals the proportion of electrophoretic bands which individual i shares with individual j. Since it is convenient to have β_{ij} and β_{ji} equal, the most natural definition of β_{ij} is

$$\beta_{ij} = \frac{1}{2} \cdot (S_{ij}/n_i + S_{ij}/n_j),$$

where n_i and n_j denote the number of bands exhibited by individuals i and j, respectively, and S_{ij} is the number of bands that the two have in common. It should be noted that any practical determination of S_{ij} requires criteria for a match to be declared between two bands. Such declarations can be intuitive, following visual inspection of the gel, or can result from checking the bands for a predefined maximum distance. In any case, it cannot be taken for granted that matching bands represent DNA fragments that are identical in size and chromosomal location. Nevertheless, Honma and Ishiyama [2] made precisely this assumption and calculated expected band-sharing rates for various degrees of kinship. These rates were found to depend solely on the average frequency (q) of alleles generating an electrophoretic band, and under the model employed by the authors, band and allele become synonymous. However, the validity of the formulae listed in *Table 5.1* depends critically upon the extent to which nonallelic DNA fragments co-migrate and thus occupy indiscernible positions on a gel.

Table 5.1: Expected band-sharing rates (β) depending on kinship

Kinship	Expected β ($\times \ 8-4q)^{a}$	β for $q = 0.1$
Sibs	$4+5q-6q^2+q^3$	0.584
Parent/offspring	$4+4q-4q^2$	0.574
Grandparent/offspring and halfsibs	$2+10q-10q^2+2q^3$	0.381
Nonrelatives	$16q-16q^2+4q^3$	0.190

[a]All figures listed must be divided by $8-4q$ in order to obtain the correct β value.
Data derived from Ref. [2].

The formulae of *Table 5.1* can be used to calculate the likelihood of a pair of DNA fingerprints, given a particular relationship between the corresponding individuals. It is reasonable to assume that the number of shared bands follows a Bernoulli distribution with parameters n_i (or n_j) and β_{ij}. From the Bernoulli distribution, the likelihood of S_{ij} out of n_i bands actually being shared is easily determined. However, for these calculations to be valid it is necessary that linkage and allelic association between the contributing loci are negligible. Therefore, in the paternity testing of trios it appears sensible to restrict the analysis to bands present in the child but not the mother. Since all such bands must originate from the true biological father, no two of them can be allelic, and the implicit assumption of independence of bands receives further support.

5.2.2 Likelihood calculations

Since the likelihood ratio is an optimal criterion for decision-making in paternity cases, most quantitative approaches represent attempts to formulate a likelihood analog for the full DNA fingerprint of a nuclear family [3,4]. To this end, a tiny grid is assumed to be superimposed upon the DNA fingerprint and to intersect it (*Figure 5.3*). Then multilocus DNA fingerprinting of trios is equated with the sampling from the eight joint phenotypes possible at a single, grid-defined gel position (e.g. child (C)+, mother (M)+, father (F)+, if all three exhibit a band at the position of interest; C+, M+, F−, if only the father lacks a band).

Appearance of a band at a gel position is regarded as the result of a Bernoulli experiment, with the probability of a band being present equal to x and that of being absent equal to $1-x$. It is further assumed that bands are transmitted independently from parents to offspring in such a way that x remains constant over generations. In order to yield meaningful results, the actual grid spacing and the number of unoccupied grid positions should be defined so that parameter x approximates to the average band-sharing rate β between unrelated individuals. Mutations creating

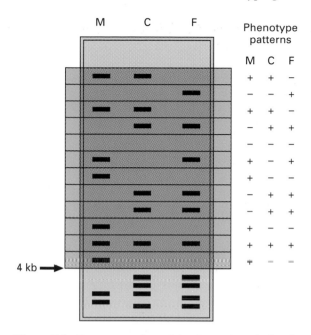

Figure 5.3: Representation of the formal analysis of multilocus DNA fingerprints. A grid is superimposed upon the autoradiograph, ranging from the largest resolvable fragments down to 4 kb. The size thresholds for the analyzable region depend on the DNA probe and restriction enzyme used. Phenotype patterns are coded at each position as + (band present) and − (band absent). M, mother; C, child; F, father.

new bands in a DNA fingerprint are dealt with by consideration of the conditional probability, w, of a band being present at a single grid-defined position in the offspring DNA fingerprint, given that it is lacking for both parents.

Position-wise likelihoods, L, for the eight possible phenotypes of a trio comprising child, mother and father are listed in *Table 5.2*. In these formulae, parameter r denotes the probability of nontransmission of a band:

$$r = [(1-x)^{\frac{1}{2}} - (1-x) \cdot (1-w)^{\frac{1}{2}}]/x.$$

In the case of false paternity, only the maternal phenotype is relevant to the child's phenotype. Thus, the likelihood under the hypothesis of non-paternity equals the product of the likelihood of the alleged father's phenotype and the sum of the likelihoods assuming that the true biological father either exhibits a band or not. For example, the likelihood of pattern C+M+F+ is

$$x \cdot [L(C+M+F+) + L(C+M+F-)],$$

assuming that the alleged father F is not the true biological father.

Although different probabilities (including zero for some patterns) have been assigned to the position-wise phenotypes by different authors,

Table 5.2: Phenotypic likelihoods at single, grid-defined DNA fingerprint positions

Phenotype[a]	Likelihood (L)
C + M + F +	$x^2 \cdot [1 - r^2]$
C − M + F +	$x^2 \cdot r^2$
C + M − F +, C + M + F −	$x \cdot (1 - x) \cdot [1 - r \cdot (1 - w)^{1/2}]$
C − M − F +, C − M + F −	$x \cdot (1 - x) \cdot r \cdot (1 - w)^{1/2}$
C + M − F −	$(1 - x)^2 \cdot w$
C − M − F −	$(1 - x)^2 \cdot (1 - w)$

[a]C, child; M, mother; F, biological father.
Data taken from Ref. 4 with permission from VCH.

independent sampling has been invoked by most of them. This assumption was made in order to calculate an overall likelihood of a DNA fingerprint as the product of the position-wise likelihoods. It receives theoretical justification from the fact that, for all loci contributing to a multilocus DNA fingerprint, only a minor proportion of alleles is actually scored. This is illustrated in *Figure 5.4* for two loci, D11S859 and D22S265, that are detected by the multilocus oligonucleotide probe (CAC)$_5$, and that have been characterized in more detail [5]. The majority of fragments are smaller than 4 kb, a figure that represents a lower limit for the resolution of individual bands in standard gel electrophoresis. Thus, most (CAC)$_5$-hybridizing bands will not be used as a source of information and this, in turn, reduces the chance of allelism and linkage for the remainder. In *Figure 5.4*, for example, the mother has only two alleles in the analyzed region (1a and 2a), whereas the father has only one (2a). Neither paternal allele of D11S859 is scored.

Position-wise independence is a problem even when the loci contributing to a multilocus DNA fingerprint are statistically independent; that is, if there is neither linkage nor allelic association. This is because the number of gel positions occupied by a band is limited (and will rarely exceed twice the number of loci involved). Thus, any concentration of bands in one region of a gel reduces the chance of finding a band in another, which implies that position-wise phenotypes are in fact not independent from each other. Furthermore, the proportion of bands an individual can transmit to an offspring is approximately 50%, so that transmission of one band slightly reduces the chance of transmission of any other.

Consequently, critics of the quantitative analysis of DNA fingerprints have targeted their attack at the independence assumption, saying in one way or another that it causes a divergence between the model and the unknown genetic reality. Although this statement is undoubtedly correct, empirical data and simulation studies have shown that it is of minor practical importance [6]. Furthermore, the relevance of these arguments depends on the relative size of the analyzed proportion of a DNA fingerprint (the 'window').

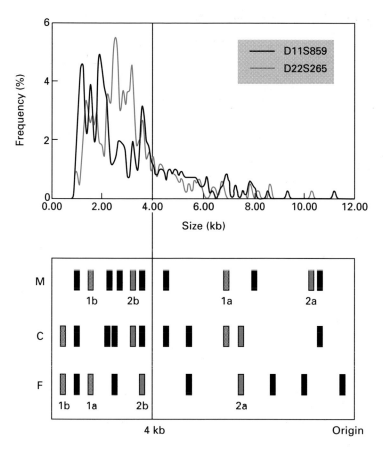

Figure 5.4: Size distribution and scoring of the alleles of loci D11S859 (coded by 1a and 1b) and D22S265 (2a and 2b), contributing to a multilocus DNA fingerprint generated with oligonucleotide probe (CAC)$_5$. M, mother; C, child; F, father.

Finally, a number of surveys of solved paternity cases have revealed that the ratio of the numbers of unassignable and nonmaternal offspring bands clearly discriminates between fathers and nonfathers. Although this ratio is smaller than 0.25 in most cases of true paternity, where unassigned bands can only result from new mutations, it was found to exceed 0.5 in the majority of false paternities both for probes 33.6 and 33.15 [5] and for oligonucleotide probe (CAC)$_5$ [7]. This implies that, even if a theoretical background for the statistical analysis of multilocus DNA fingerprints were completely lacking, empirical data based on a sufficiently large number of cases would allow practical application.

References

1. Elston, R.C. and Stewart, J. (1971) *Hum. Hered.,* **21,** 523.
2. Honma, M. and Ishiyama, I. (1990) *Hum. Hered.,* **40,** 356.

3. Evett, I.W., Werret, D.J. and Buckleton, J.S. (1988) *J. Forens. Sci. Soc.,* **29,** 249.
4. Krawczak, M. and Bockel, B. (1992) *Electrophoresis,* **13,** 10.
5. Hundrieser, J., Nürnberg, P., Czeizel A.E., Metneki, J., Rothganger, S., Zischler, H. and Epplen, J.T. (1992) *Hum. Genet.,* **90,** 27.
6. Krawczak, M., Böhm, I., Nürnberg, P. *et al.* (1993) *Forens. Sci. Int.,* **59,** 101.
7. Jeffreys, A.L., Turner, M. and Debenham, P. (1991) *Am. J. Hum. Genet.,* **48,** 824.

Further reading

Cavalli-Sforza, L.L. and Bodmer W.F. (1971) *The Genetics of Human Populations.* Freeman, San Fransico.

Ott, J. (1991) *Analysis of Human Genetic Linkage* (2nd Edn). Johns Hopkins University Press, Baltimore.

Chapter 6

Further development - technical and ethical issues

6.1 Technical improvements

The ideal system for DNA fingerprinting, or profiling, that would fit all purposes has not yet been found. All available typing systems have both advantages and disadvantages (*Table 6.1*). Future developments should thus aim at an optimization of probe design. Multilocus systems, for example, should allow positive identification of all allelic bands present in the individual under investigation, and each band should correspond to a single allele only. The efficacy of PCR technology could be improved further. If it were possible to obtain amplification products of larger size, the amount of information that could be obtained and analyzed in a single run would increase. Nonisotopic detection systems replacing radio-isotope-based probes should be simplified. Both probe- and PCR-based systems should be automated step-by-step, eventually with laboratory robots carrying out the analysis. With automated sequencing becoming cheap and commonplace, this approach may become routine for the identification of biological specimens.

Table 6.1: Available typing systems and their range of applicability

	Technical simplicity	Informative-ness	Geno-typing	Paternity testing	Works on degraded DNA?	Works on mixed samples?
Probe systems						
Multilocus	+ +	+ + +	−	+ + +	−	−
Single-locus	+ +	+ +	+	+ +	+	+ +
PCR systems						
Minisatellites	+ +	+	+	+	+	+
Microsatellites	+ +	+	+ +	+	+ +	+
Mitochondrial DNA	+	+ +	+ + +	−	+ +	−

Modified from Ref. [1].

A promising approach to a more efficient analysis of genetic variability is two-dimensional (2D) DNA typing, a technique that offers the possibility of assessing a genome in its entirety rather than at only a few sites. Originally, two-dimensional electrophoresis was developed for protein analysis and was used particularly for detecting variable patterns of individual proteins, during differentiation for example. The first successful attempt at 2D-DNA typing was undertaken by Fisher and Lerman [2] in experiments with *Escherichia coli*. Although this technique has improved substantially in the meantime, the strategy has remained unchanged. Following digestion with a particular restriction enzyme, DNA fragments are first separated according to size by standard gel electrophoresis (see Section 2.1). The gel lane containing the separated DNA fragments is then excised and transferred to a second gel containing a gradient of denaturants, such as formamide and urea. In the denaturing gradient, DNA molecules migrate until they reach a point where the two strands separate and retard further migration. The point in the gel at which the DNA strands separate depends on their base composition. Thus, 2D-DNA fingerprinting allows the simultaneous characterization of both the size and sequence of DNA fragments. After blotting and hybridization with a multilocus DNA probe, a pattern of spots results that is highly specific for the combination of the probe and enzyme used and the individual being typed.

The analysis of the hybridization patterns which result from 2D-DNA fingerprinting is more complex than the analysis of those from standard gel electrophoresis. Most of the problems noted in Section 5.2 for multilocus DNA fingerprints also apply in this instance, but the difficulties encountered in comparing results from different gels and/or different laboratories is exacerbated by the second dimension of electrophoresis. Sophisticated image analysis and database management systems are thus required in order to evaluate 2D-DNA fingerprints.

Verwest and co-workers [3] used 2D-DNA fingerprinting with four micro- and minisatellite core probes to scan for DNA variations in 10 breast cancers. In contrast to Southern blot analyses, where only a few alterations were identified, a considerable number of changes were observed in the 2D-DNA fingerprints. Most of these changes (74%) were losses of spots, consistent with the loss of heterozygosity frequently encountered in tumor tissues, and 20% consisted of amplified spots of higher signal intensity. Only in 5% of cases did a new spot become apparent. Thus, the system appeared highly efficient for detecting tumor-specific changes.

6.2 Legal and ethical considerations

With respect to individual specificity, DNA fingerprinting is comparable to its namesake, the analysis of the patterns formed by fingertip ridges. However, there is a difference in principle between these two techniques which makes DNA fingerprinting a much more important issue for ethical and social debate. Classical fingerprints may tell us with high accuracy whether a given suspect has left them at the scene of a crime or not, but this is feasible only as long as a second fingerprint is or has been taken from the accused in front of a witness. This is the case because, as yet, no means or measures have been found to correlate classical fingerprints in the general population with personal characteristics such as, for example, sex, race or population background (the fingerprint features characteristic of some clinical syndromes, such as Down syndrome, may be disregarded in this context). The nineteenth-century scientist Sir Francis Galton, who was the first to develop systems for fingerprint analysis, was concerned by this apparent drawback [4]. However, the lack of association with any important features ensured that the taking of a fingerprint did not interfere with personal privacy. This is not the case for DNA fingerprints (and profiles). All of an individual's genetic heritage is embodied in the DNA of each ordinary cell, and modern molecular genetic techniques allow this information to be retrieved very efficiently. Although determination of the complete DNA sequence is not yet feasible, a considerable amount of specific genetic data will be obtained each time an individual is typed for one of the DNA systems discussed in this book. Even if no obvious association is known between an apparently neutral polymorphism and a phenotypically important trait at the time the DNA is analyzed, it is quite possible that relevant correlations may be detected later. It is almost impossible to prove formally that a given chromosomal region has no functional importance, and molecular biologists are increasingly aware that putative 'junk' DNA may well turn out to bear a gene or another functionally relevant element.

This is especially the case for the increasing number of genes which are found to harbor triplet repeat arrays that are expanded in inherited disorders. Huntington disease, for example, a neurodegenerative disorder manifesting around the fourth decade of life, is due to the increased size of a $(CAG)_n$ repeat array in a gene located on human chromosome 4. Martin-Bell syndrome, the most frequently inherited mental disorder in European and North American countries (with a carrier frequency of around 1%), results from the expansion of a $(CGG)_n$ array (from 40–50 to more than 200 copies) in the vicinity of the X-chromosomal gene FMR1 (fragile X mental retardation). These and other disease-causing repeat expansions would have been prime candidates for detection in DNA fingerprints, using, for example, a synthetic oligonucleotide including the corresponding triplet.

Although officials may never stop professing themselves willing to avoid the use of disease-associated polymorphisms, it may nevertheless be tempting to look for new associations once the databases have been established. Eric Lander of Cambridge, MA, cautions that a closer look at a large stock of DNA data may result in statements such as 'This allele, at this locus about which I know nothing, tends to come up in rapists' (Ref. 4, p. 13). Although without any meaningful interpretation, such random findings could then be misused to nominate suspects in an increasingly close-meshed genetic net. The fact that some US states are considering, or have already started collecting DNA profiles from certain categories of convicted offenders may show that this concern is more than mere fantasy [4]. One solution would be to destroy or invalidate the data or samples stored in the context of a particular case after the case has been solved. In some instances, however, this may go against the interest of the tested individual because verification of experimental or statistical results would then become impossible after the event. It should be noted that the problem of unexpected information is not limited to DNA systems alone but may also arise with protein polymorphisms. For example, allele A of the gene encoding the ABO blood group has long been known to be associated with stomach cancer. Multilocus DNA fingerprinting is less likely than single-locus results to unravel individual-specific details involuntarily because the assignment of bands to alleles to loci is much more difficult when using multilocus probes compared to single-locus probes. This apparent drawback in the context of forensic and kinship testing turns out to represent a welcome inbuilt protective device against the misuse of genetic data. Results of multilocus DNA fingerprinting consist of the more or less computerized documentation of banding patterns (i.e. phenotypes) rather than of genotypes. Thus, without any direct access to the DNA (i.e. the original electrophoretic gel), a multilocus DNA fingerprint cannot yield data on disease association.

In 1966, the California Supreme Court decided that physical evidence should not be protected against self-incrimination [4]. Thus, suspects in California have no right to refuse to donate body material, such as blood, in contrast to verbal evidence which they can refuse to provide. This decision was obviously made in order to balance individual rights with the public demand for a functioning system of criminal prosecution. It follows from the Universal Declaration of Human Rights (adopted by the UN General Assembly on 10 December 1948) that there are many things a state should simply not be allowed to do, such as torture, no matter how useful they are thought to be from the viewpoint of truth seeking. The presumption of innocence, basic to the legal systems of most countries, further serves to protect the individual against the power of the state. However, excluding from forensic practice molecular biological techniques capable of delivering powerful evidence of guilt may well burden a society with more costs than would any associated restriction of individual rights. In other words, in a stable nonauthoritarian society, there may be more to fear from criminals than from a misuse of DNA data by the state and its agencies. Although this argument appears agreeable at first sight, it nevertheless ignores the fact that political conditions are subject to permanent change. Whether governments keep their word or will be able to do so in the future cannot be certain.

Similar arguments apply to databanking. Whereas the mutation rates of most repetitive DNA systems are sufficiently low that multiple mismatches in DNA fingerprints are equivalent to an unequivocal exclusion of donorship, positive proof requires a comparison of the matched sample to a reference population. Without databases, the impact of DNA profiling as a means of positive identification would be limited. Although this problem may be overcome in the forseeable future by the use of DNA sequencing techniques, questions about randomness can be answered at present only by means of population genetics.

Even when the state is exonerated from any misuse of DNA data, other potential interested parties remain which are likely to demand access to this kind of information. A knowledge of the health risks of particular clients or employees can be seen to be particularly beneficial to insurance companies and employers. This development proceeds on the back of man's unique efforts to uncover completely his own genetic inventory. The Human Genome Project (a concerted international effort to map and sequence the entire human genome) has already unravelled new disease–marker associations and will ultimately lead to identification of the DNA sequences involved. Technological improvements allowing cheaper, faster and more efficient genetic analyses will also result from this project. Together with the initiation of population-wide screening programs for people affected by, or with a genetic predisposition towards, some common inherited disorders such as cystic fibrosis and Martin-Bell syndrome, the Human Genome Project may thus emphasize the need to protect genetic data.

We should like to point out that the high efficiency and reliability of DNA profiles must not lead to over-interpretation of their meaning. Positive identifications are still based on probabilities, and statistical analyses always provide information about uncertainties rather than about facts. Furthermore, the large odds often reported in the context of DNA fingerprinting, such as one in a billion or even one in a trillion, have no meaningful interpretation since the empirical observations on which they are based are usually so few that juggling with such arithmetic monstrosities is by no means justified. Finally, it should not be forgotten that even proof of identity, and that is all DNA fingerprinting can at best achieve, does not necessarily constitute proof of guilt.

References

1. Jeffreys, A.J., Monckton, D.G. and Tamaki, K. (1993) in *DNA Fingerprinting: State of the Science* (S.D.J. Pena, R. Chakraborty, J.T. Epplen and A.J. Jeffreys, eds). Birkhäuser Verlag, Basel.
2. Fisher, S.G and Lerman, L.S. (1983) *Proc. Natl Acad. Sci. USA*, **80**, 1579.

3. Verwest, A.M., de Leeuw, W.J.F., Molijn, A.C., Andersen, T.I., Börresen, A.L., Mullaart, E., Uitterlinden, A.G. and Vijg, J. (1994) *Br. J. Cancer,* **69,** 84.
4. Rabinow, P. (1992) in *DNA on Trial* (P.R. Billings, ed.). Cold Spring Harbor Laboratory Press, Cold Spring Harbor.

Appendix A. Glossary

Alleles: alternative forms of a gene. Alleles reside at the same locus but differ with respect to DNA sequence.

Allelic association: tendency of particular alleles of different genes to occur in the same genotype.

Amino acid: building blocks of peptides (proteins). Amino acids share the same basic structure but have different side groups.

Autosome: chromosome other than a sex chromosome (X and Y in humans). Autosomes are present in homologous pairs in practically all nucleated cells.

Bayes' rule: mathematical formula for calculating posterior probabilities of alternative hypotheses by combining associated information with prior odds.

cDNA: DNA complementary to mRNA, synthesized from RNA by an RNA-dependent DNA polymerase.

Ceiling principle: in identification of suspects by DNA fingerprinting, a controversial attempt to deal pragmatically and conservatively with unsound allele frequency estimates and population differences. Instead of an actual frequency estimate, use of either its maximum, taken over a number of different populations, or a fixed value (e.g. 5%) is recommended, depending on which of the two is larger.

Centi-Morgan (cM): unit of genetic distance. Two loci are said to be 1 cM apart if they recombine, on average, once per hundred meioses.

Centromere: cytogenetic structure of a chromosome to which the spindle fibers become attached before cell division and chromatid separation.

Chiasma: temporary contact and regional overlap of different chromosomes, chromatids or parts of the same chromosome.

Chromatid: one of the two subunits of a duplicated, but not yet separated, chromosome. Chromatids become visible at certain stages of meiosis and mitosis.

Chromatin: ensemble of DNA, proteins and RNA that constitutes the genetic material of a cell not in the process of division.

Chromosome: packaged DNA; an assembly of linearly grouped genes and extragenic sequences. Chromosomes become microscopically visible as distinct structures during cell division.

Chromosome complement: the set of chromosomes present in a somatic or germ cell.

Clone: a cell population derived from the same ancestor cell.

Codon: a nucleotide triplet (DNA or RNA) specifying an amino acid.

Coefficient of selection: relative measure of the selective disadvantage of a given genotype or phenotype.

Cross-hybridization: hybridization between DNA and/or RNA of different species due to sequence homology.

Crossing-over: process of breakage and reunion that results in the exchange of genetic material between different chromosomes or chromosomal regions.

Deamination: chemical reaction which results in the replacement of amino by hydroxyl groups.

Depurination: removal of purines (adenine and guanine) from the phosphodiester backbone of the DNA.

Dideoxynucleotide: nucleotide containing dideoxyribose instead of ribose or deoxyribose. A dideoxynucleotide can be added on to a growing DNA chain by DNA polymerase, but then prevents further elongation.

Diploidy: presence of two complete sets of chromosomes.

DNA: deoxyribonucleic acid.

DNA polymerase: enzyme that catalyzes the synthesis of DNA.

DNA probe: short piece of DNA which, after labeling, is used as a detection device in molecular hybridization experiments.

Dominance: ability of an allele to express a particular trait in heterozygotes.

Dot blot: analytical method in which an aliquot of the test substrate (RNA or denatured DNA) is spotted on to a membrane to be subsequently analyzed, for example, by hybridization with a specific probe.

Electrophoresis: separation of charged molecules in an electric field.

Epistasis: interaction of genes where particular alleles of one gene interfere considerably with the phenotypic expression of another gene or genes.

Eukaryote: an organism the cells of which contain a nucleus.

Exon: segment of a gene that codes for a part of a polypeptide.

Fixed bin: category of DNA fragments, classified by length, with fixed upper and lower borders.

Floating bin: category of DNA fragments, classified by length, with upper and lower borders depending on the length of a given reference DNA fragment.

Founder effect: increase in frequency of an otherwise rare allele due to its presence in a small founder population.

Gamete: mature reproductive cell capable of fusing with another gamete.

Gene: a functional unit of DNA sequence which encodes either a protein or an RNA species.

Gene expression: phenotypic manifestation of the function of a gene.

Gene flow: migration of specific alleles from one population into another.

Genome: entirety of the genetic material in a cell, its nucleus or its organelles.

Genotype: genetic information implied by either a single locus, a group of loci or the entire genome.

Germline: lineage of cells ancestral to a gamete.

Glioma: a brain tumor.

Haploidy: presence of one complete set of chromosomes, including one sex chromosome.

Haplotype: particular alleles of a given set of genes present on one chromosome.

Hardy–Weinberg law: mathematical formulae that, under idealistic conditions, allow genotype frequencies to be computed from allele frequencies.

Heterozygosity: presence of two different alleles of a given gene in a diploid cell.

Homozygosity: presence of two identical alleles of a given gene in a diploid cell.

Infinite allele model: a mathematical model to explain the size distribution of VNTR alleles.

Intron: gene segment that does not encode a polypeptide. Introns are removed from the initial RNA transcript of a gene by a splicing process to yield mature mRNA which contains only exon sequences.

Karyotype: chromosome complement of a particular individual or group of related individuals.

Linkage: tendency of loci in physical proximity to exhibit co-inheritance of their alleles. Loci with a meiotic recombination rate significantly smaller than 0.5 are said to be linked.

Linkage disequilibrium: allelic association due to close linkage.

Locus: the physical position of a gene on a chromosome or genetic map.

Marker: a DNA sequence of known location within the genome.

Meiosis: the two final cell divisions during gametogenesis leading to haploid germ cells.

Mendelian locus: locus at which the inheritance follows the rules first recognized by Gregor Mendel.

5-Methylcytosine: chemical modification of cytosine that is liable to transition into thymine. In vertebrates, 5-methylcytosine occurs predominantly in CG dinucleotides.

Microsatellite DNA: repetitive DNA with repeat size ranging from 1 to 6 bp and a repeat copy number per locus of less than 100.

Minisatellite DNA: repetitive DNA with repeat size ranging from 9 to 100 bp and a repeat copy number per locus of less than 1000.

Mitochondrion: small semi-autonomous organelle of the cell (100 to several thousand copies per cell).

Mitosis: cell division that results in two daughter cells, both of which are genetically identical to the other and the parental cell.

Molecular hybridization: formation of a DNA–DNA or DNA–RNA duplex *in vitro*.

mRNA: messenger RNA. A gene is transcribed to yield RNA which is then processed to produce mRNA. The mRNA codes for a specific polypeptide.

Multilocus probe: DNA probe that is complementary to more than one locus.

Mutation: alteration of quantity or sequence of the genetic material due to exogenous or endogenous causes.

Nucleic acid: deoxyribonucleic acid (DNA) and ribonucleic acid (RNA).

Nucleotides: building blocks of nucleic acid, consisting of one of the five organic bases adenine (A), guanine (G), cystosine (C), thymine (T) or uracil (U) (the latter replacing T in RNA), a sugar molecule (ribose in RNA, deoxyribose in DNA), and a phosphate group.

Oligonucleotide: a short sequence of nucleotides.

Oncogene: gene which may cause malignancy when mutated or improperly regulated.

Open reading frame: DNA sequence with protein-encoding potential.

Palindrome: tandem of complementary DNA sequence motifs either abutting on to each other or separated by a small number of nucleotides. The recognition sites of almost all restriction enzymes are palindromic (e.g. CTGCAG for *Pst*I).

Panmictic: mating at random. In a panmictic population each individual is equally likely to mate with a given individual of the opposite sex.

Phenotype: observable properties of an organism, resulting from the interaction of genetic and environmental factors.

Polymerase chain reaction: a process which yields enzymatic amplification of DNA *in vitro*.

Polymorphism: co-occurrence of at least two different alleles of a gene, both at a frequency greater than 1%, in a given population.

Polypeptide: a covalently linked chain of amino acids.

Polyploidization: the conversion of a cell or an organism from a haploid or diploid state to an increased number of complete chromosome sets per cell.

Primer: starting molecule that binds to single-stranded DNA or RNA and facilitates synthesis of a complementary strand.

Prokaryote: organism with cells, each of which lacks a nucleus.

Pseudogene: apparently functionless DNA sequence with significant homology to a functional gene, indicating a common evolutionary origin.

Recessivity: pattern that allows phenotypic expression of a particular allele in the homozygous state only.

Recombination: process of exchange of genetic material between different chromosomes or chromatids.

Reproductive fitness: parameter that is proportional to the reproductive success (i.e. number of offspring) of an individual of a given genotype.

Restriction enzyme: enyzme with endonucleolytic activity that enables bacteria to recognize and degrade foreign DNA.

Restriction site: short DNA sequence which a restriction enzyme recognizes and at which it cuts double-stranded DNA.

Retrotransposition: process of reintegration of RNA-encoded genetic information into the genome of a cell.

Reverse transcriptase: a DNA polymerase which catalyzes the synthesis of DNA using RNA as a template.

RNA: ribonucleic acid.

Satellite DNA: repetitive DNA with both repeat size and repeat copy number per locus above 1000.

Segregation analysis: statistical methodology aiming at elucidating the genetic model (e.g. number of genes, number of alleles or mode of inheritance) underlying a particular phenotype.

Selection: differential, non-random reproduction of individuals of different genotypes.

Single-locus probe: DNA probe that is complementary to and hybridizes to only one locus in the genome.

Slipped (strand) mispairing: mutational mechanism invoked to explain deletions and insertions. Mispairing of single-stranded DNA occurs during replication and is mediated by repetitive and palindromic sequences.

Southern blot: transfer to a membrane of DNA molecules separated by gel electrophoresis.

Somatic: related to cells other than germ cells and their precursors.

Telomere: end of a chromosome.

Transcription: synthesis of RNA molecules using DNA as a template.

Transition: substitution of a purine for a purine (A to G, G to A), or a pyrimidine for a pyrimidine (C to T, T to C).

Translation: synthesis of polypeptides according to the information embodied in mature mRNA.

Transversion: substitutional mutation changing a purine (A, G) into a pyrimidine (C, T) or vice versa.

Unequal crossing-over: crossing-over between improperly paired homologous chromosomes or chromatids.

Yule coefficient: numerical measure of allelic association.

Zygote: in eukaryotes, cell formed by the fusion of two germ cells.

Index

ABO blood group, 3, 38, 67, 73, 92
Adenocarcinoma
  gastrointestinal, 59
Adult polycystic kidney disease, 37
Agarose gel, 20, 24, 69
Allele, 2
  distribution, quasi-continuous, 31, 70
  dominant lethal, 45
  frequency, 30, 45, 62, 75–76
    chance fluctuation, 73
    equilibrium, 43–44
    estimation 63, 74
    stability, 45
  length, 31, 71
    interchromosomal difference, 28
  neutral, 45
  number, 30, 58
Allele-specific oligonucleotide (ASO),
  25, 28
Allelic association, 30, 45, 63–65, 70, 81,
  84
Allelism, 36, 86
Alu repeat family, 15, 51–52
Amino acid, 4, 6, 10
Amish, 46
Amphibian, 13
Amplification fragment length
     polymorphism (AmpFLP), 69
Aplastic anemia, 38
Arthropods, 38
A-rule, 56
Autoradiograph, 85
Autosome, 8–9, 36

Bacteria, 4
Bacteriophage M13, 33

Band
  allelic, 83, 89
  independence, 84
  intensity, 32–33
  position, 32
  resolution, 86
  tumor-specific, 59
Band-sharing, 83–84
Base
  organic, 4
  pair, 5
Bayes' rule, 66–67
Bernoulli distribution, 84
Bin
  definition, 83
  fixed, 70–71
  floating, 70–73
  frequency, 71
  phenotype, 72
  size, 70
Binning, 70–74
Biological trace, 61
Blood
  group, 43, 74–76
  stain, 72
Bone marrow, 38

Cambrian, 48
Cancer, 59
  breast, 90
  molecular etiology, 37
  stomach, 92
Carbon atoms
  numbering, 5
Carcinogenesis, 59
Ceiling principle, 76

101

ORDERING DETAILS

Main address for orders

BIOS Scientific Publishers Ltd
St Thomas House, Becket Street,
Oxford OX1 1SJ, UK
Tel: +44 865 726826
Fax: +44 865 246823

Australia and New Zealand
DA Information Services
648 Whitchorse Road, Mitcham, Victoria 3132, Australia
Tel: (03) 873 4411
Fax: (03) 873 5679

India
Viva Books Private Ltd
4346/4C Ansari Road, New Delhi 110 002, India
Tel: 11 3283121
Fax: 11 3267224

Singapore and South East Asia
(Brunei, Hong Kong, Indonesia, Korea, Malaysia, the Philippines,
Singapore, Taiwan, and Thailand)
Toppan Company (S) PTE Ltd
38 Liu Fang Road, Jurong, Singapore 2262
Tel: (265) 6666
Fax: (261) 7875

USA and Canada
Books International Inc
PO Box 605, Herndon, VA 22070, USA
Tel: (703) 435 7064
Fax: (703) 689 0660

Payment can be made by cheque or credit card (Visa/Mastercard, quoting number and expiry date). Alternatively, a *pro forma* invoice can be sent.

Prepaid orders must include £2.50/US$5.00 to cover postage and packing for one item and £1.25/US$2.50 for each additional item.